Praise from Around the World for *A Writer's Toolkit*

"If you ever want _____ _____ _____ _____ _____ _____e talking about, give them an exa_____ _____ _____ay: Oh, so *that's* what you mean. That's _____ _____ Carroll Dale Short brings to *A Writer's Tool K____*. ____hen he talks about transitions, he *shows* you transitions. When he talks about pruning pronouns or narrative, he *shows* you these things. And that's a lot more powerful than *telling* us about them. I defy anyone, including myself, to read this book and not learn a lot about writing." —CLARKE STALLWORTH, former editor, *The Birmingham News*

⟡

"Any writer, novice or seasoned, will benefit from reading Carroll Dale Short's *A Writer's Tool Kit*. Those who master his 'dozen tested, proven approaches,' will cut their years of agony in half. I heartily recommend it—even to readers who simply wish to enhance their appreciation of good writing." —IBRAHIM FAWAL, author of *On the Hills of God*

⟡

"I believe *A Writer's Tool Kit* will be especially useful for the motivated high-school student. It serves as a valuable resource with uncomplicated and useful advice, and it also

serves as encouragement: a good and trusted friend with which to replace the irritating 'internal critic' we all face as writers—an especially intimidating force when one is young."
—JANET MEGO, Advanced Placement English teacher, Walker County (Alabama) High School

       ⊷⚬⊶

"*A Writer's Tool Kit* is a reader's tool kit, too. When I see an Olympic diver go off the board, all I can say is, "Wow, he didn't make much of a splash." Someone who knows about diving, whether or not they do it themselves, will appreciate every little angle and twist. I want to have the same kind of understanding when I read a book. How does the writer do it? Short provides the answers here, with clarity, brevity, and wit." —RUTH BAVETTA, San Bernardino (California) Junior College

       ⊷⚬⊶

"My brother won troubleshooting contests in Auto Mechanics class. Me? I almost put a quart of oil in the radiator. Or was it a gallon of water in the crankcase? But when it comes to writing, Short gives us the whole kit—not only the conceptual tools for writing, but how to troubleshoot when we have problems.Short's writing experience has run the gamut—from strict AP-style news to feature stories, magazine articles, short stories, essays, poems, novels, plays, technical manuals, and creative non-fiction. It's apparent from *A Writer's Tool Kit* that he genuinely cares about other writers, and wants to pass on what he himself has learned from other people. —LYDIA SMITH, American Studies Program, University of Alabama

"So you want to be a writer? *Yes*. It can be a hard journey over treacherous terrain. *Oh*. No dishonor to cut across every chance you get. *Where?* Well, this man Short has been there and back, and in his *A Writer's Tool Kit* are true ways as real as William Carlos Williams's 'red wheelbarrows' and 'white chickens' that will save you years and pain." —JOHN LOGUE, author of *Life at Southern Living*

"I'm always trying to make my students aware of the rules, patterns, tricks of the trade—call 'em what you will— that will improve their work and make it more palatable. Experience shows that those who develop such an awareness have a head start over the rest of the field. That's where Dale Short's *A Writer's Tool Kit* comes in. He presents a 'dozen tested, proven approaches,' some of which he arrived at 'by trial and error' (often the best way!), some acquired from 'an array of gifted and dedicated teachers.' We all know what the golden rules are. Go easy on modifiers. Don't waffle. Involve the reader. Be specific. Keep it simple. In other words, *get on with it! Tell the story!* Easy to remember, not always so easy to put into practice. Will *A Writer's Tool Kit* help? Surely, if you take the time to digest its examples, then the benefits will be yours, whether you're a raw beginner or a seasoned pro. — IAN MARKS, teacher, Uddingston, Scotland

"Mr. Short states his intention to present the reader of this book twelve rigorously honed tools for strengthening the reader's own writing. He then proceeds with wit, humility and down-to-earth good humor to construct with his own finely crafted writing a presentation case for these tools that is the prime example for each of the twelve.

"At the same time he gives gentle lessons for recognition of these tools in works from a wide array of authors and a guide for successfully incorporating these applications to the writer's own projects. I recognize in this effort his own habits of reading and exploration in the world of words. His clear though not clinical delineation of the use of these tools would be of value to anyone who writes, whether writing for one's own eyes in journal-keeping, writing for class work at any level and particularly in any course teaching writing skills and writing for publication—including established writers looking for fresh insights. So prepare to choose and use your tools: whether you apply transitional glue, make frequent use of the pronoun pruner, or learn the patience needed for boiling down your prose to its refined essence."
—BEATRICE SOILA, teacher, Helsinki, Finland

"Not only is the writing refreshingly clear, but *A Writer's Tool Kit* makes wonderful sense. This is the sort of book that teachers need and will love. In the best possible way it demystifies the writing process, taking you, the reader and aspiring writer, with it every step of the way. Along with Robert Pirsig's *Zen and the Art of Motorcycle Maintenance*, *A Writer's Tool Kit* is essential reading for the thinking reader and writer." —CASSIE FLINT, teacher, London, England

A WRITER'S TOOL KIT

12 Proven Ways
You Can Make Your Writing
Stronger—Today!

CARROLL DALE SHORT

Court Street Press
Montgomery

Court Street Press
P.O. Box 1588
Montgomery, AL 36102

Library of Congress Cataloging-in-Publication Data
Short, Carroll Dale
A writer's tool kit : 12 proven ways you can make your writing
stronger--today / Carroll Dale Short.
p. cm.
ISBN 1-58838-045-9
1. English language--Composition and exercises. 2. English
language--Rhetoric.   I. Title: Writer's tool kit, twelve proven ways
you can make your writing stronger--today. II. Title.
PE1408 .S48765 2001
808'.042--dc21
2001047380

ISBN 1-58838-045-9

Design by Randall Williams
Printed in the United States of America

A Writer's Tool Kit has a companion web site at
http://www.writerstoolkit.com

To the Memory of
MRS. PEARL HUFFMAN
World's Greatest English Teacher,
Who Graced the Lives of the Students
of West Jefferson (Ala.) High School
from 1933 to 1966

And to the Memory of
JESSE HILL FORD
Writer, Craftsman, Mentor, and Friend

CONTENTS

Introduction

There are a ton of hard-and-fast rules about writing, but you won't find any of them in this book. What you *will* find in *A Writer's Tool Kit* are exactly one dozen tested, proven approaches to making your writing sing, instead of croak or sputter.

Where did these concepts come from? A few, I arrived at sheerly by trial and error and frustration over the past thirty years of making a living by writing. Most of them, though, I gained in person from an array of gifted and dedicated teachers with whom I have been blessed since my childhood. Some of those teachers—including the two to whom this book is dedicated—have already passed on, and none of their teachings exist, that I know of, in any written form.

One thing I can say with total confidence is that every writer's education is ultimately self-education, and, as such, is a supremely personal and singular predicament. There is the ever-present possibility that the very next thing you hear from a teacher, or read in a book, or painstakingly figure out for yourself in isolation at the keyboard, will suddenly fire up that metaphorical, cartoon light bulb inside your head, at which time you have an "Ah-HAH!" moment, which no less a writer than James Joyce has dubbed an "epiphany."

At that point, you will have discovered the exact thing about the process of writing that *you* personally most need to know at that stage of your writing life, even though other students around you may not be particularly impressed. These other writers have their own trajectories, their own epiphanies. Bless them, wish them well, give thanks to your teacher, and move on.

The twelve tools in this book—it being, after all, a tool kit—have been rigorously honed, refined, and improved not only on my own battered keyboard, but also by thousands of writers in seminars I've taught around the country over the past thirty years, and to whom I'll be forever grateful for their gifts of thought, discovery, and validation.

I've arranged the sections roughly in order of their significance and applicability to the most different types of writing. But because all writers are different (and more than a wee bit independent sorts, God bless 'em), you should feel free to begin *A Writer's Tool Kit* by browsing, or even starting at the end and reading backwards. (Not literally, of course.)

Furthermore, depending on how many years you've been at this writing biz, you may well find a tool that you've already mastered. More power to you. But as some anonymous sage has said, "Half of learning is the process of reminding ourselves of what we already know."

And, one final caveat. Raise your hand, please, and repeat after me:

"I will not think about any of the stuff in this book *while* I am trying to write." The reason is simple. Writing any-thing, from scratch, is a daunting enough task without having to keep a bunch of tips and how-to's bouncing around in your mind as well.

In fact, most writers will tell you that the single hardest thing they learned to do is to keep their mind *empty* of everything except the story they're trying to tell at the time.

The principles in *A Writer's Tool Kit* are for *after* you've finished your first draft. Miracle of miracles, you've taken some blank pieces of paper and turned them into a narrative engine that actually runs on its own fuel. All it needs now is a tune-up. Or two. That's what the tools in this book are for.

I hope you enjoy the journey.

Transitions:
The Basic 'Glue' of Good Writing

Most of us write (and read, and speak) transitions all day long, lickety-split, without giving them much thought. But in actuality, these low-profile building blocks of effective writing are one of the most important tools of all in keeping a reader's interest and attention from Page 1 to the end.

What's a transition? It's any word, phrase, sentence, or paragraph that bridges the space from one type of thought to another, without changing the subject.

Transitions glue together paragraphs, essays, feature articles, chapters, and entire books—the more seamlessly, the better.

And is a transition. So is *but*. (A little trade secret, here—no matter what you may have heard from antiquated grammarians—both *and* and *but* are just fine for beginning sentences with. Try them and see. Nobody will whack you with a ruler. And your readers will thank you.)

Slightly more complex transitions are:

—*Not only that, but . . .*

—*To make matters worse . . .*

—*On the other hand . . .*

—*Unbeknownst to Fred, though . . .*

—*Before this whole thing started . . .*

Transitions, especially in fiction, are one of our most effective tools for handling the passage of time, which is not always as easy as it looks.

Transitions range from the simple and straightforward to the elaborately complex. Here's a fairly straightforward one from Ernest Hemingway's *The Sun Also Rises*:

> By that time, though, he had other things to worry about. He had been taken in hand by a lady who hoped to rise with the magazine. She was very forceful, and Cohn never had a chance of not being taken in hand. Also he was sure that he loved her.

But for pure simplicity, it's hard to beat the time-passing transitions in Knut Hamsun's landmark—and stylistically influential—1921 saga *Growth of the Soil*:

> Time passed. Spring. Summer. Autumn.

See? It's all in the way you hold your wrist.

To get a better grasp of the crucial role that transitions play in a narrative, let's look at a style of writing in which transitions are not just unwelcome, but are forbidden.

This form of writing with the strangely restrictive rules can be found with surprising ease: just pick up your nearest newspaper.

The "straight," or "hard" news stories that newspapers receive from wire services such as Associated Press are written in a style known to journalists as the "inverted pyramid" format.

The job of the first paragraph is supremely straightforward. Namely, to give the reader—without preamble or verbal throat-clearing—the famous "five W's" of the news reporting profession: who, what, where, when, and why.

For example, AP reporter Yuri Bagrov writes in a story datelined Nazran, Russia:

> Four Russian soldiers were killed when rebel fighters ambushed a military unit in central Chechnya in the second attack on a convoy in two days, an official said Saturday.

Who, what, where, when, and why—all in a single sentence. The second paragraph adds more details:

> The convoy was fired upon Friday while moving through the Vedeno Gorge, a region that has seen heavy rebel activity since the start of the war, according to an official with the pro-Russian civilian government in Chechnya.

The third paragraph does more of the same:

> The official, who spoke on condition of anonymity, did not have further casualty figures. The attack was one of 12 carried out by the rebels in the last 24 hours across Chechnya, the official said.

Likewise for the fourth, fifth, six, etc., and on to the end. Picture a pyramid, balanced upside-down on its point. Now envision repeatedly slicing this pyramid horizontally into a stack of thin sections.

The top slice, which is the largest, contains what the writer discerns as conveying the most *important and comprehensive* pieces of information about the event he or she is reporting on.

The second slice, not quite as large, contains the *next most important* facts about the event. And likewise, on down the end of the pyramidal food chain, whether the article contains ten paragraphs or forty.

As familiar as the style is to us as readers, it's a formal and demanding one. Why no transitions, though?

The reason is pragmatic: the news business is all about deadlines. Depending on the type of publication, a given editor may have only a few hours—or in some cases, just minutes—to digest a mountain of factual information from around the world and decide (a) which stories to use, (b) their relative ranking in importance to the reader, and (c) how best to fit those stories, along with any photographs, illustrations, and headlines, into the exact amount of space remaining for editorial matter after the advertisements have been put into place.

Imagine adding to this pressure-cooker situation by having to rewrite stories on the fly, making them longer or shorter to fit the exact rectangular "hole" in which they're put. This is where the inverted pyramid comes to an editor's rescue.

Stories written in the strict style of the inverted pyramid format offer what journalists sometimes jokingly call "news by the yard." Because each paragraph is self-contained, and there are no transitions or other dangling loose ends, an editor can cut the story to exact size, after the end of any paragraph, and know that the story will still make sense.

A busy reader, likewise, can take in the headline, and choose to read as many paragraphs of a wire-service story as his or her interest in the subject demands.

Not all journalism is written in this style, of course. There are also pieces known as "feature" or "color" stories, and they differ from so-called "straight" news in matters of writing style and approach, rather than the relative importance of the subject matter.

With the benefit of a day's thought and reflection, for instance, a newspaper often assigns one day's headline story to a feature reporter for a piece in the next day's edition— same subject, different style. Instead of a straightforward presentation of facts, the feature writer can bring to the story not only the perspective of hindsight but also include descriptions and sensory impressions, afterthoughts of participants, overheard conversations, earlier related incidents that may have precipitated the big story, and so on.

In other words, by thoughtfully sequencing these elements and others—with the liberal use of our good friend, the transition—the writer can convert factual information into a *story*, or narrative (in the next chapter, we'll look more closely at some of the factors that make narrative style different), with a traditional beginning, middle, and end.

In our age of growing information overload, we often crave the *story*, with its gift of context, as much or more than we do the initial *news* of the event. Especially when a news item involves a personal tragedy, our question of "What happened?" once satisfied, then changes to "*How* could this have happened?" And it's here that the old-fashioned talents of basic storytelling come into play.

Feature writers often must pay a high price for that freer rein and extra day or two of breathing room, however. Feature stories generally are written to a predetermined word-length, to fit the space that has been set aside by an editor or layout designer. A writer might be told, for instance, "We've got the top half of page two, so you need to make it 1,500 words."

Give or take a dozen or two, of course. But writing a narrative to exact length can still be a daunting task. One wise person has compared it to "putting together a jigsaw puzzle on a moving turntable."

The matters of writing to length, abridging, and compression are all very important subjects in themselves, and we'll examine those skills in greater detail in Chapter 7.

In the meantime, though, the overall message is an encouraging one. Having to shoehorn a certain story into a certain space can serve not only to strengthen its structure and enhance its prose style, but it can also be one of the most valuable learning exercises a writer can engage in. In short, it's a win-win situation for us keyboard toilers.

One contemporary virtuoso of the feature-story style is Pulitzer-winning reporter Rick Bragg, who works for *The New York Times*.

Observe how Bragg opens this report, written in the wake of the 1998 school shootings in Jonesboro, Arkansas, where two boys ages eleven and thirteen shot dead four of their classmates and a teacher, and wounded ten others:

> This is a place that has learned to cherish a slow day.
>
> Most days, Dennis Woody and the other paramedics at Emerson Ambulance have a nice, long wait between calls, and sit talking on the soft, secondhand sofa, watching television, thinking about how they could throw darts at the dartboard, if they really wanted to.
>
> On Tuesday, an afternoon that forever altered the lives of so many in this small city, Mr. Woody found himself on his knees in a blood-spattered schoolyard, trying in vain to make a young girl live again as her father stood over him and chanted, "Come on, come on, come on."

Most days, T.J. Kelley of radio station KFIN cracks jokes, reports on soybean futures, and spins country music ballads for lovesick teenagers, helping to heal broken hearts that are never really broken all that much. This week, he tries to help young listeners who feel guilty for just being alive while their classmates and friends are dead from a hail of bullets, and pours words out onto the airwaves that remind this place how good and decent it was before this, and will be again.

Most days, Mitchell Faught, who has run the flower shop for 34 years, and Grover Cooper, longtime superintendent of schools, join other older men in the McDonald's to drink coffee, read newspapers, and joke about Mr. Cooper's impending retirement.

This morning, as four of his students and a teacher lay in funeral homes and two young schoolmates sat in jail, charged in the killings, the talk was kinder than usual.

"How you doing, Grover?" Mr. Faught asked.

"I'm going to be fine," Mr. Cooper said.

Most people here say that. They will be fine, only different...

The repeated, low-key litany of transitions that Bragg uses to introduce his narrative are so naturally skillful that a reader of this piece is likely to overlook them, the first time through. But in fact, invisibility is the highest compliment that can be paid a transition.

Look again at the contrasting, almost call-and-response

openings of the series of alternating paragraphs, which—while being as comfortable as a conversation between old friends—set up the theme of the piece in a structure that will continue until the end, when the paragraphs' openings suddenly reverberate in an unexpected way:

> Most days...
> On Tuesday...
> Most days...
> This week...
> Most days...
> This morning...

These simplest of transitions offer the ideal framework for what this particular story is about: the unimaginable contrast between "then" and "now," in the lives of real people, after a tragedy of such proportion. The rhythm of the alternating setup allows the storyteller to introduce, almost coincidentally, some information that his research has turned up: prior to the school shootings, the people of the town of Jonesboro's worst collective memory was a 1983 schoolbus wreck in which eight people died.

"A tragedy," Bragg writes, *"but a thing that they could understand."*

Bragg proceeds to work in (in a relatively short space) more images, sensory impressions, perspective, and behind-the-scenes detail than a viewer of CNN, or of most other broadcast outlets, received while riveted to the so-called "main story," including this unflattering section:

> What they are losing respect for, say many here, is the news media. The first mass invasion of news media here has been an ugly one for many people. Two television camera people cursed each other outside the county jail because one had gotten in the way of the other's shot.
>
> Today, Sheriff Haas told reporters, some from around the world, that his switchboard was flooded with complaints from people here. Television trucks block driveways and access roads. Some reporters have refused to leave doorsteps when people asked them to, or have been trespassing or offering money for stories.
>
> "If it doesn't stop," the sheriff said, he will ask his deputies to start arresting people . . .

None of this, thanks to Bragg's journalistic objectivity, is his personal opinion, but rather the "story," as he hears various and conflicting parts of it told, by fellow human beings.

And the writer's closing of the report is, fittingly, an echo of the same transitions that have powered it from the beginning:

> . . . But mostly, people have gone about the necessary things in this bad time. Mr. Faught, the florist, usually does about 75 arrangements a day. Today, he and his workers did more than 200. The orders for the funerals are

still coming in.

People here say the city is small enough so names and faces are familiar, and history seems to circle around itself. In the bus accident of 1983, one passenger, a man named Terry Woodward, was credited with saving the lives of several students.

Mr. Woodward is the stepfather of 13-year-old Mitchell Johnson, one of the two boys sitting in jail, blamed for the killing of his classmates.

Bragg's relatively short (1,520-word) article is not only a well-told story of a complex and world-headline-grabbing local tragedy, but it also confronts the irony and mystery of the human situation in elegantly simple language.

From the viewpoint of his fellow writers, the piece is also a testament to the astonishing flexibility of the literary device known as a transition. Not only can the device work as narrative Super-Glue, it can also at times serve as the very fuel which powers a story from beginning to end, as well as filling many other technical roles in between.

Suffice it to say, for now, that "transitions" are one of the heftiest and most-used wrenches in an effective writer's tool kit.

2

The 'Punch' of Effective Storytelling: It's All a Matter of Time...ing

Ask any stand-up comedian. (Or actor, or athlete, or dancer, or musician, or orchestra conductor, or track coach.) Timing is everything. There are situations in which the smallest fraction of a second, virtually negligible to an ordinary state of consciousness, can literally make or break your performance.

The same is true of writing winning prose, though the applications and parallels are far more nebulous and generally less understood.

Let's break the subject of timing down, going from narrow view to broad view.

A sequence of syllables makes up a word. A sequence of words makes up a sentence. A sequence of sentences makes up a paragraph. A sequence of paragraphs makes up a story (or essay, or article, or book, or what-have-you).

In our study of timing, though, it's helpful to keep in

mind the familiar term "punch line." A punch line, in comedy, is a crucial piece of information—whether a sentence, a phrase, a word, or even a physical gesture—that is purposefully saved until last.

That's because the punch line serves to "detonate" in the listener's mind all the other information that has preceded it, casting that information in some new light. This detonation may take the form of surprise, outrage, confirmation, enhancement, deja vu, or any number of other reactions—all of them leading to laughter, either hearty, nervous, or somewhere in between.

As an example, take any joke that comes to mind (from classic to corny), change the sequence of the information, and see what happens.

Comedian Emo Phillips:

"My parents moved a lot, when I was growing up. But I kept finding them."

Rephrased, "No matter how many times my parents moved off and left me, when I was growing up, I kept finding them." A sad and troubling statement, maybe, but by no means a joke—*i.e.*, something we would react to by laughing.

Laughing and crying, smiling and wincing, snickering and choking up, are forms of emotional release. And the effective narrative sets up this emotional release by carefully withholding and revealing information in just the right *sequence* for maximum impact, like springing a trap that has been set beforehand.

Every good paragraph has a punch sentence. Every good sentence has a punch word.

(Do words have punch syllables? Well, sort of. But we'll get to that in a moment.)

An example of a sentence with a punch word?

Try this one by Anne Lamott, from her memoir *Traveling Mercies: Some Thoughts on Faith,* about her young son's reluctance to attend Sunday morning church services:

> "Let's go, baby," I say cheerfully to Sam when it is time to leave for church, and he looks up at me like a puppy eyeing the vet who is standing there with the needle.

Rearrange the order of the words in that deceptively simple sentence, and try to find a more effective punch word (no pun intended) than "needle."

E.B. White, the *New Yorker* essayist probably best known for his children's classic *Charlotte's Web,* was not only a gifted prose stylist but a master of timing as well. In his essay "The Death of a Pig," White describes his surly old dachshund's perverse joy over the failing health of the family's pig:

> He never missed a chance to visit the pig with me, and he made many professional calls on his own; you could see him down there at all hours, his white face parting the grass along the fence as he wobbled and stumbled about, his stethoscope dangling—a happy quack, writing his villain-

ous prescriptions and grinning his corrosive grin.

As for examples of paragraphs with punch sentences that go straight to the heart, it would be hard to improve on these two, once again from the duo of Anne Lamott and E.B. White. Lamott, in *Traveling Mercies*, reflects at one point:

> It's funny. I always imagined when I was a kid that adults had some kind of inner toolbox, full of shiny tools: the saw of discernment, the hammer of wisdom, the sandpaper of patience. But then when I grew up I found that life handed you these rusty bent old tools—friendships, prayer, conscience, honesty—and said, Do the best you can with these, they will have to do. And mostly, against all odds, they're enough.

And White, in his essay "The Ring of Time," writes about the spontaneous beauty of watching circus performers at a summer rehearsal—ordinary people with a talent, practicing in comfortable clothes in plain daylight, unsullied for the moment by the refinements of makeup and spotlights and sequined costumes. Here, he describes a sixteen-year-old girl standing balanced on the back of a horse as it gallops around a ring:

> The richness of the scene was in its plainness, its natural condition—of horse, of ring, of girl, even to the girl's bare feet that gripped the bare back of her proud and

ridiculous mount. The enchantment grew not out of anything that happened or was performed but out of something that seemed to go round and around and around with the girl, attending her, a steady gleam in the shape of a circle—a ring of ambition, of happiness, of youth. In a week or two, all would be changed . . . the girl would wear makeup, the horse would wear gold, the ring would be painted, the bark would be clean for the feet of the horse, the girl's feet would be clean for the slippers that she'd wear. All, all would be lost.

In that single paragraph, White conjures such a wealth of images and action that the writing seems to take on the amazing energy of a child's spinning top, which slowly, slowly, winds down until it finally topples—and we see that the finely sharpened point that had borne the top's whole rotating weight, throughout the sequence, was a single word:

Lost.

⤙═◉═⤚

As for the broader picture—the subject of timing over an entire piece of prose—one of the most basic principles is that your beginning and ending paragraphs should contain some of your very strongest writing.

This holds true whether that entire piece of prose is self-contained (a magazine article, an essay or short story within a collection), or is one of many segments in a larger, encompassing piece of work—one chapter of many in a book, for example.

In the shorter form (essay, story, article), you as a writer have two basic objectives— (1) to entice a browsing reader of a larger publication into reading *your* particular contribution to same, based on the opening paragraph alone—and then (2) leaving him/her with a final paragraph that literally resounds with a summary of your story that echoes forward into the reader's thoughts, after the publication has been laid down.

You open strong, you end strong. Good job!

In a book-length piece of writing, however, another variable comes into play. That's because the end of each chapter is a natural stopping point for the reader to take a break and lay the book down—maybe to return to it again, maybe not.

The equivalent of a chapter's end, for television producers, is the commercial break. That's why producers, over the years, have honed the art of the narrative "hook": a new piece of information in the story, an old piece of information suddenly seen in a new light, a question raised, or a deepening of complications and consequences that up the emotional ante for both the characters and the audience. If the hook works successfully, the viewer will have accumulated enough interest to wait out the commercial in order to see what happens next.

In its most basic (*i.e.*, least subtle) form, a narrative hook resembles the "cliffhanger" scenario of the old weekly movie serials—so named because the scene often consisted of a hero literally hanging by his fingernails to a high precipice, with no rescue in sight. Or, alternately, the damsel-in-distress theme, said damsel tied to a railroad track with a speeding train bearing down.

Fortunately, chapter breaks don't require a literal cliffhanger, of the old school (though it certainly couldn't hurt). What they *do* require is good, basic storytelling at work.

For example, what reader of Jonathan Harr's powerful nonfiction book *A Civil Action* isn't at least tempted to turn to the next page by his strong chapter endings? The book tells the story of a lawyer's struggle, against tremendous odds, to get justice for a small New England community whose residents are dying of leukemia due to big corporations' reckless release of toxic wastes into their water supply.

In Harr's scene below, lead attorney Jan Schlichtmann and his associate Kevin Conway are planning strategy late at night, after a particularly bad day in court:

Schlichtmann and Conway were the last to leave the office that evening. It was near midnight. "What do you think, Kevin?" Schlichtmann asked as they walked out the door together. "Should I have been more haranguing?"

Conway looked thoughtful but he didn't answer directly. "Riley surprised me today," he said. "He came off looking better than he should have. He was so arrogant and combative in his deposition."

"He's a liar but he's not stupid," said Schlichtmann.

Conway nodded as he put on his coat. "I think you've got to get angry, Jan."

As the court battle with the chemical company Goliath drags on, Schlichtmann and his associates fall millions of dollars into debt, pledge their cars and the deeds to their houses as collateral, and are still harassed daily by creditors—with the law firm's faithful accountant, Gordon, often rushing to the rescue with just enough finagled cash to keep the electricity from being cut off or their office computers repossessed.

Then, out of the blue, a bit of good luck. A small past case—medical malpractice, unrelated to the chemical poisonings—suddenly reactivates when an insurance company offers to settle out of court. Desperate for cash, the partners agree to accept the offer. But their satisfaction is fleeting:

One of the insurance adjusters left the room to make a telephone call. When he returned, he took Schlichtmann aside and said the company that made the anesthetic used in the operation had agreed to contribute ninety thousand dollars to the settlement. The offer was now five hundred ninety thousand. Was that enough?

This time, Schlichtmann and his partners left the room to consult in private. When they came back, Schlichtmann poured a glass of whiskey and proposed a toast.

Schlichtmann's firm received 40 percent of the settlement. In the past, a payday of this sort would have been cause for celebration, dinner out for the entire staff at an expensive restaurant, bonuses all around, and a night of drinking and revelry. But there was no party that night. The entire fee would have to go directly to pay bills. The money would disappear as soon as it arrived.

As the lawyers' prospects, and those of the leukemia victims' families, grow more and more grim because of unexpected setbacks in the case, the partners disagree on whether to quit and take the settlement that's offered them, or press to the end with a jury deciding the verdict:

Conway went into the bedroom to pack. After a few minutes Schlichtmann followed him into the room, still carrying the glass of wine. Conway hefted his suitcase on the bed and took off his suit jacket and folded it. Schlichtmann, his arms crossed, leaned against the door and watched him, saying nothing.

"It's over, Jan," said Conway as he packed. "If we go on, it'll destroy us all. We've got to stop it now."

Schlichtmann still didn't say anything. He shrugged and then turned and left.

Conway watched him go. He knew the case wasn't over until Schlichtmann said it was. When Schlichtmann was out of earshot, Conway said to the others, "He's willing to take everything a step further than anybody else.

God knows, he loves the edges. If he decides to go to trial, I'll be there. But I hope he doesn't. God, I hope he doesn't."

Strong narrative way-stations such as these make it more difficult for the reader to bail out of the journey without knowing what happens next . . . and next . . . and next. The story keeps drawing us ahead until, before we know it, we're at the end of the book. That's good narrative structure—and good narrative *timing*—doing its job.

⋯⟨⊙⟩⋯

Chapters with punch paragraphs. Paragraphs with punch sentences. Sentences with punch words.

Words with punch *syllables*? Why not?

Writers and storytellers have known for centuries that their audience responds strongly—albeit viscerally, at a level below conscious thought—to certain *internal rhythms* of the words that make up a sentence.

Ray Bradbury tells the story of sitting in his den listening, many years ago, to a recording of Dylan Thomas reading his own poetry. Some of the poems were complex, and Thomas's thick accent and distinctive cadence required Bradbury to focus his total attention on the recording so as not to miss any of the words.

At one point, Bradbury noticed that his daughter—four

years old, at the time—had come into the room and stood off to one side, listening to Thomas's reading as if hypnotized.

When the recording reached its end, the girl turned to her father and said, "Wow, Dad . . . that guy sure knows what he's doing."

"She couldn't have understood one word out of three," Bradbury remembers. "I think what had reached her from Thomas's reading was the *sound* of the language, the rhythms of it. She knew intuitively that there was a power, an authority, there."

And it's no coincidence, I maintain, that the root word of "authority" is *author.*

Whether we hear the words of a poem or narrative spoken aloud, or read them silently to ourselves, the *sound* of those words is nonetheless imprinted on us at some deep level, and that sound plays a large role in how we interpret the *content* of what we're reading or hearing.

As readers, we say that certain authors are "great stylists," or that they have "a lyrical voice," or "a fine-tuned ear for the language."

The term "lyrical" comes from the Latin for "lyre," a musical instrument—and appropriately so, since prose has much in common with music.

Just as certain musical scales have become standardized over the years because, for whatever reason, they "sound right" to human beings, particular rhythms of language have become favorites of poets and other writers. The basic elements of these rhythms are "stressed" and "unstressed" syllables.

High-school literature class introduced us to two of the most common of these forms, the *iamb* (an unstressed syllable followed by a stressed one, as in the words "delay" or "about"), and the *trochee* (a stressed syllable followed by an unstressed one, as in "country" and "rabbit").

When we discovered Shakespeare, we also discovered the curious fact that, from the bewildering array of other forms available, this unthinkably prolific writer chose a single metrical form—iambic pentameter, or five iambic "feet" in a row— for virtually all of his work ranging from sonnets to plays.

> Shall I compare thee to a summer's day?
> Thou art more lovely and more temperate:
> Rough winds do shake the darling buds of May,
> And summer's lease hath all too short a date...

Why iambs? Why pentameter? Who can say? But on hearing it, we know at once that it *sounds* good. It's a form that gives majesty and grace to his language—whether the subject is a gentle love poem, as above, or a stirring pep-talk by a king to his greatly outmanned army, as in Shakespeare's play *Henry V:*

> We few, we happy few, we band of brothers;
> For he to-day that sheds his blood with me

Shall be my brother; be he ne'er so vile,
This day shall gentle his condition:
And gentlemen in England now a-bed
Shall think themselves accurs'd they were not here,
And hold their manhoods cheap while any speaks
That fought with us upon Saint Crispin's day . . .

There's a magical, other-worldly energy and authority in those lines—enough to make even a good pacifist want to grab a sword and crack some skulls.

And while the meter of prose is not as formal and regimented as poetry, we can still hear the echoes of those majestic rhythms in such writing as the descriptive passages of Joseph Conrad's classic story "Typhoon," in which the crew of a steamship are besieged in the China Sea by a historic and monstrous storm:

As soon as he attempted to open the door the wind caught it. Clinging to the handle, he was dragged out over the doorstep, and at once found himself engaged with the wind in a sort of personal scuffle whose object was the shutting of that door. At the last moment a tongue of air scurried in and licked out the flame of the lamp.

Ahead of the ship he perceived a great darkness lying upon a multitude of white flashes; on the starboard beam a few amazing stars drooped, dim and fitful, above an immense waste of broken seas, as if seen through a mad drift of smoke.

> On the bridge a knot of men, indistinct and toiling, were making great efforts in the light of the wheelhouse windows that shone mistily on their heads and backs. Suddenly darkness closed upon one pane, then on another. The voices of the lost group reached him after the manner of men's voices in a gale, in shreds and fragments of forlorn shouting snatched past the ear . . .

Even if these lines were in a language unrecognizable to us, I believe we would still comprehend—as did Bradbury's young daughter in the unfamiliar brogue of Dylan Thomas—that this was an author of great skill and purpose, who was intently telling us about something immediate and important.

Though Conrad is long dead, his voice on the page carries a distinct authority. *That guy knows what he's doing.*

Compare Conrad's resounding lyricism to, say, a passage of dry legalese which is written strictly to convey information, without the need to hold an audience:

> This agreement does not cover repair of any product which is damaged or malfunctioning due to causes beyond the manufacturer's control including, but not limited to, repairs necessitated by owner negligence, improper installation, accidental damage, abuse, vandalism, theft, rust, animal or insect infestation, and acts of nature.

Obviously, there's no easy formula for producing writing that "sounds good." But if we can generalize at all about rhythm in prose, it seems that a reader craves a pattern of words that is somewhere between the random and the artificially forced. As readers, we respond best to a give-and-take of syllables, word length, and sentence length that sounds, and feels, as if it were created with meaning and purpose—or as if it had existed all along in the natural world, like ocean waves or a bird's song.

Consider, despite a tone completely different than Conrad's, the narrative authority of the opening paragraphs of Mark Helprin's novel *Winter's Tale*:

> There was a white horse, on a quiet winter morning when snow covered the streets gently and was not deep, and the sky was swept by vibrant stars, except in the east, where dawn was beginning in a light blue flood. The air was motionless, but would soon start to move as the sun came up and winds from Canada came charging down the Hudson.
>
> The horse had escaped from his master's small clapboard stable in Brooklyn. He trotted alone over the carriage road of the Williamsburg Bridge, before the light, while the toll keeper was sleeping by his stove and many stars were still blazing above the city. Fresh snow on the bridge muffled his hoofbeats, and he sometimes turned his head and looked behind him to see if he was being followed. He was warm from his own effort and he breathed steadily, having loped four or five miles through

the dead of Brooklyn past silent churches and shuttered stores. Far to the south, in the black, ice-choked waters of the Narrows, a sparkling light marked the ferry on its way to Manhattan, where only market men were up, waiting for the fishing boats to glide down through Hell Gate and the night.

But language that sounds "good" or "commanding" doesn't necessarily translate as "pretty" or "fancy." There's a beauty in bleakness, too, as this passage from Cormac McCarthy's novel *All the Pretty Horses* demonstrates:

> He rode with the sun coppering his face and the red wind blowing out of the west. He turned south along the old war trail and he rode out to the crest of a low rise and dismounted and dropped the reins and walked out and stood like a man come to the end of something.
>
> There was an old horse skull in the brush and he squatted and picked it up and turned it in his hands. Frail and brittle. Bleached paper white. He squatted in the long light holding it, the comicbook teeth loose in their sockets. The joints in the cranium like a ragged welding of the bone plates. The muted run of sand in the brainbox when he turned it.
>
> What he loved in horses was what he loved in men, the blood and the heat of the blood that ran them. All his reverence and all his fondness and all the leanings of his life

were for the ardenthearted and they would always be so and never be otherwise.

By this point, in our discussion of "timing," somebody is probably thinking, "Oh, great. Besides all the other stuff I have to think about when I'm writing, now I have to worry about how everything *sounds*."

Not at all. Please refer, again, to our implied contract in the introduction of this book: our goal, as writers—particularly during a first draft—is to keep our conscious mind *off* everything except the story we're attempting to tell. Going through a page of writing, counting *iamb*s and *trochee*s and trying to divvy them up consistently from sentence to sentence, would be a recipe for disaster. Sound, rhythm, and pacing are *intuitive* functions, the words and their order supplied to us from our aural imagination, or what someone has called our "inward ear."

But even our intuition can benefit from a jump-start. The best way to develop a graceful, melodic style of writing is to read authors whose styles you admire and whose writing *sounds* and *feels* most natural to your inward ear. Many writers I know, myself included, find that the time just before sleep is a particularly fertile one for what Jesse Hill Ford called "priming the pump": mentally ingesting the images and rhythms of good writing into your subconscious, to be processed and transformed during sleep and, with grace and luck, to be reborn the next morning as a gentle momentum of new images and rhythms that power you past the initial obstacle of a blank page.

(An underground phenomenon I've discovered among writers is that many of us have found a "totem" book or author we use as a sort of first-aid kit—reading a page or two before we do our own writing, to help clear our minds of the dissonance of everyday reality. Ford swore by an obscure— and narratively cryptic —novel by Marguerite Young titled *Miss Macintosh, My Darling*, and it's become my standby as well. Anywhere I might dip into its 1,450 pages, I find vivid, fantastic images relayed in lyrical language, which set my imagination and "sound-sense" careening off in new directions of their own.)

Don't be afraid that, by priming your imagination's pump on the words of another writer, you're somehow *imitating* him or her—a concern I've found especially prevalent among younger or beginning writers. A writer's style is such a complicated mix of factors that it's virtually impossible to reproduce exactly. Witness the popularity of annual events such as the "Faux Faulkner" and "Imitation Hemingway" contests, and more recently "Not-McCarthy," in which entrants attempt to copy the three authors' prose styles.

One of the main attractions of these competitions based on the work of such distinctive stylists is that the winning entries are at once familiar and . . . very funny. They tend to blur the fine line between tribute and parody, and in the process underscore the futility of copying anything more than the most outwardly noticeable traits of a writer's style.

In fact, we hear so often about a writer finding his or her "unique, individual voice" that we're led to think of the discovery as something exotic and incongruous, like coming across a perfect topaz in a bowl of oatmeal. We envision charismatic worshipers suddenly speaking in "unknown tongues," or the voice of a demon coming out of a little girl's larynx as in the movie *The Exorcist*.

The reality, though, is far less frightening (thank goodness) and more manageable (ditto). That's because the phrase "unique voice" is actually an oxymoron. If a person were capable of inventing a way of speaking and writing that was truly unique (*i.e.,* it had never been done before), then nobody would be able to understand what they were saying—in the same way that no painter has ever invented a color that hasn't existed in some form since the beginning of time, only new ways of combining them.

Writers and painters and other artists grow in skill and range by *refining* and *recombining* the various means of expression that have come before them and by which they have, consciously or not, been influenced.

For writers, that boils down to discovering, by trial and error of much writing, and after wide and omnivorous reading, a written *style* that is the clearest possible expression of their particular story's *content*. One size does not fit all, there's no single set of instructions, and the results can't be charted or diagrammed.

How do we know when a voice "works?" Because the ink-on-paper words suddenly seem to fall away, and the reader is transported into the place and time of the narrative—whether it's yesterday in Seattle, or Medieval times in rural France. Not until we come to the end and look up from the page does the "real" world reassemble itself around us.

On the one hand, it's a miracle. On the other, as we've seen in this chapter, miracles are largely a matter of . . . timing.

3

Pruning Pronouns: Getting the 'It' Out

pro·noun (pronoun´) *noun:*

Grammar. One of a class of words that function as substitutes for nouns or noun phrases and designate persons or things asked for, previously specified, or understood from the context. Examples: *he, she, it.*

Pronouns! What would we do without them? Most likely, we would write paragraphs like this one:

When a housewife, in New York or in Florida, comes home from market with a dozen eggs and opens the housewife's package, the housewife finds twelve pure white eggs. Twelve pure white eggs are, to the housewife, not only what an egg should be, twelve pure white eggs is what an egg is. An egg is a white object. If this same housewife were to stray into New England and encounter a brown egg from the store, the egg would look somehow incorrect,

45

wrong. The brown egg would look like something laid by a bird that didn't know what it was about. To a New Englander, the opposite is true.

Thanks to the gift of pronouns, though, we have this far smoother original paragraph, taken from E.B. White's essay "Riposte":

> When a housewife, in New York or in Florida, comes home from market with a dozen eggs and opens her package, she finds twelve pure white eggs. This, to her, is not only what an egg should be, it is what an egg is. An egg is a white object. If this same housewife were to stray into New England and encounter a brown egg from the store, the egg would look somehow incorrect, wrong. It would look like something laid by a bird that didn't know what it was about. To a New Englander, the opposite is true.

Much better, huh? The avoidance of repetition made possible by pronouns not only allows us (or White, rather) to shave off eleven words from the length of the first paragraph, with no loss of meaning, but also makes for a more elegant, and natural-seeming, flow of the reading experience.

That's the good news. The bad news is that pronouns are *so* handy and functional, we often tend to over-use them in our writing.

How does that over-use affect the reader? The pronoun is a literary cipher, a place-holder, into which the reader subconsciously inserts the "real" noun that precedes it, and for which it stands.

There are two catches to this convenience, and the definition tells us what they are: the nouns must be *previously specified*, or *understood from the context*.

Let's take the trickier of the two first: context.

A reader comes to each new piece of writing with absolutely zero context—except, of course, for any hints that can be gleaned from its title or headline—and builds that context cumulatively, word by word.

The *writer*, on the other hand, comes to the first blank page of a piece of writing armed with nothing *but* context— that is, a general knowledge of what the piece is to be about—and proceeds to parlay that context, brick by slow brick of words, into a coherent reading experience.

With such diametric starting points, is it any wonder that we as writers tend to presume our reader understands far more of the context than is actually the case? (Or, as Flannery O'Connor once advised writing students, "Do not attempt to be subtle until at least page four.")

Consider the most common pronouns: *He, she, it.*

The "he" and "she" are fairly straightforward, as pronouns go. If a paragraph or scene or chapter is about only one human being in solitude, then the person, after once being introduced, can afterward be referred to as a "he" or "she" until the cows come home, with no risk of confusing the reader as to who's who.

(In practical terms, a long string of "he" or "she" can

become so monotonously repetitive that we want to use the subject's name now and again, if only for the sake of variety.)

Likewise straightforward are scenes with one "he" and one "she." Unless one of the participants is actually in the midst of a sex-change, we can safely identify them through pronouns until it's time to re-state one name or the other for variety's sake.

When there's more than one "he" or "she," of course, the pronouns have to be used more sparingly so we can keep track of the players without a program. In fact, the reader subconsciously appreciates the repetition of names and other antecedents, and thus the factor is not nearly as noticeable to the reader as it is to the writer. When in doubt, err on the side of clarity. (Or as John Gardner advises, in his book *The Art of Fiction*, "The meaning of a sentence should be as obvious as a grizzly bear in a well-lighted kitchen.")

If the repetition of proper names gets to be too monotonous, we can always substitute some type of descriptive tag ("the daughter," "the stockbroker," "the longshoreman," "the swimming coach," etc.) to keep clear who's doing what.

So far, so good.

Where most writers get into trouble, though, is with the most multi-purpose, nebulous, and all-encompassing pronoun there is:

It.

Stephen King got a whole book title out of it (so to speak), but then he had to spend the next 1,093 pages telling us what *It* is. So this is clearly not a representative case.

With the pronoun "it," the catch that comes into play is the first definition, above: *previously specified*.

In the case of "he" and "she," what is previously specified obviously must be a person (okay, or an animal); so except in the instance of a mob scene, the use of "he" or "she" greatly narrows down the options of what the place-holding pronoun's antecedent can be.

With "it," though, all bets are off—which is why, for the sake of clarity in our writing, we should try to use "it" most sparingly of all and, particularly when revising something we've written, put each "it" to the most stringent tests to see if there's a better word.

"It," the master chameleon of pronouns, can refer to a place, a thing, or an idea—all of which good writing teems with, vastly outnumbering the cast of characters.

One useful test of "it" is to count backward, by the word, and determine *how many* words earlier its antecedent was mentioned. The longer the gap, the shakier the ground for justifying an "it." Also check to see if any other word appearing in that gap might be mistaken, by any stretch of a reader's imagination, for the antecedent that you intend.

To return to E.B. White's example, let's take a very up-close and detailed look (imagine the slow-motion replay of an Olympic diving event) at his choice of pronouns in these two sentences:

> If this same housewife were to stray into New England and encounter a brown egg from the store, the egg would

look somehow incorrect, wrong. It would look like something laid by a bird that didn't know what it was about.

First off, we note that the writer had an opportunity to
use the pronoun "it" in three instances, but only did so
twice: *It would look like something...* and *a bird that didn't
know what it was about.* The antecedent of the first "it" is
"egg," and the antecedent of the second "it" is "bird."

How does White rate on the matter of word-count gap
between pronoun and antecedent?

There are five words in the gap separating "it" and "egg,"
and four words in the gap between "it" and "bird." Excellent
score, and easily within the limits of an average reader's
comprehension.

(And while there can obviously be no hard-and-fast high
limit as to how many words apart a writer can place a
pronoun and its antecedent before the reader experiences
brain-clog, my gut feeling, based on experience, is that a ten-
word gap is starting to push your luck, and at a dozen or
more you should either take another look at your sentence
structure or else hope that the reader of your piece is really
paying close attention, *i.e.*, stoked on caffeine.)

Now, for the question of "to pronoun, or not to pronoun." If White made great use of "it" in the second
sentence—and twice, at that—then why didn't he do so in
the first sentence, as in:

If this same housewife were to stray into New England

and encounter a brown egg from the store, it would look somehow incorrect, wrong.

Our main clue is the "previously stated" component of the definition of a pronoun. In the structure of this sentence there are *two* possible, previously stated, nouns that the "it" could refer to: "egg," and "store." Is it the *egg* that looks somehow incorrect and wrong, or is it the *store* that somehow looks incorrect and wrong?

Based on the *context* of the usage, in light of the entire paragraph, common sense tells us that the coloration of the egg, and not of the store, somehow looks incorrect and wrong to said shopper.

Still, White chooses to forego the shortcut of a pronoun in this instance, because that shortcut would require us, as readers, to unnecessarily shift mental gears: from the simpler "previously specified" principle to the far more nebulous notion of "understood from the context," as additionally viewed through the prism of each reader's own, very individual and varying, common sense.

So, like any good architect or poker player, prose stylist E.B. White plays it smart: taking the hit of one extra word and repetition ("the egg," rather than "it") in a tradeoff for the sake of clarity.

Why so much fuss, over a tiny "it"?

As mentioned earlier, a reader's brain is a wonderful device that, totally on auto-pilot, comes to a dead halt at each pronoun for an infinitesimal fraction of a second while searching backwards—either in memory, or on the page—for the word it symbolizes, and fills in the blank before moving ahead again.

But as marvelous as the reader's fill-in-the-blank capability is, it can be overtaxed, at which point a grain of irritation forms. If enough of these grains accumulate—particularly if the cause is sloppy writing, such as improper or vague pronoun usage—the reader is likely to lay the piece of writing aside. Maybe to return to it, maybe not.

Are there exceptions to this principle? Of course.

See Henry James, Marcel Proust, Virginia Woolf, William Faulkner, Toni Morrison, Cormac McCarthy, and scores of other great writers who at times spin a complex labyrinth of language, single sentences that go on for a page or more, a veritable house-of-cards of dependent clauses, writing so dense that an intrepid reader must take it on faith—backtracking, re-reading, and pondering as necessary in order to get at the full meaning of all that is on the page.

Consider this passage from Woolf's novel *To the Lighthouse*:

> Let it come, she thought, if it will come. For there are moments when one can neither think nor feel. And if one can neither think nor feel, she thought, where is one? Here on the grass, on the ground, she thought, sitting down, and examining with her brush a little colony of plantains. For the lawn was very rough. Here sitting on the world, she thought, for she could not shake herself free from the sense

that everything this morning was happening for the first time, perhaps for the last time, as a traveler, even though he is half asleep, knows, looking out of the train window, that he must look now, for he will never see that town, or that mule-cart, or that woman at work in the fields, again. The lawn was the world; they were up here together, on this exalted station she thought, looking at old Mr. Carmichael, who seemed (though they had not said a word all this time) to share her thoughts. And she would never see him again perhaps. He was growing old. Also, she remembered, smiling at the slipper that dangled from his foot, he was growing famous. People said that his poetry was "so beautiful." They went and published things he had written forty years ago. There was a famous man now called Carmichael, she smiled, thinking how many shapes one person might wear, how he was that in the newspapers, but here the same as he had always been. He looked the same—greyer, rather. Yes, he looked the same, but everybody had said, she recalled, that when he had heard of Andrew Ramsay's death (he was killed in a second by a shell; he should have been a great mathematician) Mr. Carmichael had "lost all interest in life." What did it mean—that? she wondered. Had he marched through Trafalgar Square grasping a big stick? Had he turned pages over and over, without reading them, sitting in his room in St. John's Wood alone? She did not know what he had done, when he heard that Andrew was killed, but she had felt it in him all the same. They only mumbled at each other on staircases, they looked up at the sky and said it will be fine or it won't be fine. But this was one way of knowing people, she thought: to know the outline, not the detail, to sit in one's garden and look at the slopes of a hill running purple down into the distant heather. She knew him in that way. She knew that he had changed some-how...

This difficulty does *not* come about, however, because James, Proust, Woolf, Faulkner, Morrison, McCarthy, *et al,* are sloppy or careless writers. To the contrary: each is employing, in his or her own inimitable way, a hard-won mastery of writing style in order to convey ideas that are so subtle, complex, ineffable, and/or profound as to be virtually unsayable within the given shackles and limitations of con-ventional language. In other words, they are being as clear as they possibly can, given their material.

Sometimes they succeed, sometimes they fail. But it's the enormity of the endeavor, the richness of the however rough and challenging ride, that entices a reader into staying the course. Reading and writing tastes aside, all of this is the reason that classics are classics.

Trust me on this:

Unless you've been officially certified as the sole literary heir of James or Proust or Woolf or Faulkner or Morrison or McCarthy, your best bet by far is to go for the grizzly bear in the kitchen approach. Never make your language more complicated than it has to be under the circumstances.

Note that all of the above comments in this section apply to *written* language—that is, prose which appears in the form of sequential pages, either paper or electronic, through which the reader can flip backward or forward, at will, to re-read a specific sentence, paragraph, chapter, etc.

Far different in comprehension requirements are audiobooks (true, the listener can rewind to clear up a difficult section, but is not apt to do this repeatedly) and prose that's intended for broadcast. The latter only has one chance to get its message across to the audience—a special challenge in radio, in which the words exist on their own, without the reinforcement of video images, photographs, or charts.

For models of clear, concise, and compelling writing, in which the requirements for clear antecedents, easily decipherable clause structure, etc., are cranked up to the max, we can learn a lot from listening closely to the daily news programs on National Public Radio, such as "Morning Edition" and "All Things Considered."

As an experiment, count the number of times *he, she, it,* and *they* are used in a five-minute period. Chances are, there won't be a lot—and considerably fewer than in a comparable work for the written page.

So...

Be thankful to the English language for the wonderful gift of pronouns. But when you're writing for clarity, do as the beer and wine commercials say: enjoy them in moderation.

4

The Power of Narrative Sequence:
Making a Story 'Flow'

ell me a story. A simple enough request, and one that's been around since the beginning of human speech. And though some people are better natural storytellers than others, nearly all of us spontaneously tell stories to our children, and to one another, without a second thought.

It's only when we sit down to do it at a keyboard that we so often lose our way. Part of the problem is one of the chief demons lurking in every writer's brain: self-consciousness.

Namely, we tend to learn from years of classroom assignments that we have two chief goals in putting something on paper: (a) trying to look intelligent to whoever's going to read (and possibly grade) what we've written, which consists in large part of (b) giving the most accurate and complete information in the most logical and straightforward way possible. Or, if you will, *Just the facts, ma'am.*

Paradoxically, this basic way of writing that becomes second nature to us well before we reach adulthood is the worst, and most deadly dull way to tell a story—in fact, as we'll discover in this chapter, it's almost exactly the *opposite* of storytelling.

Technically, the art of storytelling is known as *narrative writing*, whether the narrative is fiction or nonfiction, and whether it will eventually become a book, a movie, a stand-up comedy routine, a play, an opera, or any number of other forms.

By contrast, the type of writing at which most people are skilled and comfortable is *expository writing*. And no matter how much style, intelligence, vocabulary, and even humor an expositional writer brings to his or her task, the basic goals are the same: to give the reader important information in a straightforward way.

Some common types of expository writing include legal briefs, "white papers" from industry or government committees, police reports, newspaper editorials, "hard" news stories, and technical articles in medical or academic journals. Each of these forms of exposition carries its own sizable demands, including a keen knowledge of the audience for each piece and their expectations, a grasp of proper style, form, jargon, and so on.

The art of storytelling is—again, paradoxically—both far easier in some ways than expositional writing and far more difficult in others. Let's look at some examples:

I used to deer-hunt a lot. But I quit, ten or eleven years ago. I'm still not sure exactly why.

I have a very clear memory of the last deer I killed. It

was a cold morning and the ground was wet and frozen and I was smoking a cigarette when I saw him through the trees, a six-pointer. A beauty. I put the crosshairs of the rifle scope on his chest, got as steady as I could, squeezed the trigger, and he went down. I didn't have to shoot him again. He only thrashed for about ten seconds.

I field-dressed him and brought him home, and we took pictures of him. I still have one of the pictures. I'm wearing my cowboy boots and holding the deer's head up by his horns, while our two little puppies prance around me. My hair is down in my face. I look a lot younger than I do now.

That was the last deer I ever killed.

Not a bad little sequence of prose, huh?

But a narrative, it's not. What it *is* is a brief passage that I took from Larry Brown's powerful memoir, *On Fire*, and rewrote it, as straightforwardly and accurately as I could, into a piece of *expositional* writing.

Now, compare it to Brown's original (and condensed just a bit, for length purposes) *narrative*:

The ground is wet and frozen and my butt is wet. I sit smoking the cigarette, the rifle across my lap. In the creek below me I see yellow horns move and I drop the cigarette from my fingers and look at him. He is standing there, testing the wind with his nose. The white patch of his throat, his tail down, not alarmed at all.

I count the six points on his head and raise the rifle out of my lap in extra-slow motion and move it toward my shoulder as he swings his rack, as he stands in the creek in his world and doesn't know that I'm here. I don't look into his black eyes. That would alarm him and he'd run. The sun is out and it's ten-thirty as I lay the crosshairs on his chest.

I want to kill him dead, with one shot. He's the most beautiful thing I've ever seen besides my babies. The crosshairs rest steady on his chest and I try to calm myself, not to dread the slap of the rifle. I hold it firmly and touch the trigger gently, fire, clap of sound, slap of the rifle all instantaneous, and he goes down. He kicks hard in the leaves. I don't want to shoot him again. It hurt me bad enough to shoot him the first time.

In less than ten seconds the thrashing dies down. I hold the scope on him and look. Jesus Christ. I've killed him. He lies dead. He's the biggest one I've ever killed. He suffered some. But he didn't suffer a lot. He felt confusion and then died. Would that we could all do that, when it comes.

I took the deer home and we took pictures of him. There is one that remains, me in my cowboy boots holding the deer's head up by the horns, two little puppies that will later die of parvo prancing around him, my hair down in my face, a much younger guy than I am now. That's been ten or eleven years ago, and I haven't killed another deer since then.

Some people probably wouldn't think of these things as nearly a religious experience. But I felt God in my trigger finger that day, in the way the deer lifted his horns and tested the wind, trying to smell and see me, where I was sitting so still and so small against that little tree, smoking a cigarette, almost ready to go home.

⋅❖═◉═❖⋅

Let's look at some of the differences in these two pieces of prose.

For one thing, the expositional version *begins* with the *ending* of this series of events, which to some extent lets the reader off the emotional "hook" up front. Do the words "thesis paragraph" ring a bell with anyone who's ever done a school report? We're taught to condense, and/or synopsize, what you're about to say to the reader, up front, to emphasize its importance and how it will be addressed throughout your piece of writing.

By contrast, Larry Brown's narrative follows one person's perceptions and reactions, moment by moment, with the ending unknown until the very last lines. So, it's safe to say that a main thrust of narrative writing is not the *supplying* of total information about a situation, but rather the *purposeful withholding and unfolding* of those facts and information in ways that make emotional and instinctive—though not necessarily logical—sense. The chief characteristic of a story, as opposed to a synopsis, is to leave the reader wondering what is going to happen next.

Please note, though, that our finest storytellers are *not* withholding this factual information in any manipulative, or sneaky, fashion, for an unwarranted surprise or cheap thrill like hearing fair-goers shriek at one last surprise drop-down witch at the end of a fun-house ride.

Some suspense writers, however—and some surprisingly prominent ones, not to mention any names—actually *cheat.*

There, I said it.

Let's say you're reading along in a suspense novel for several chapters, trustingly limited to the viewpoint of the main character's consciousness, and then you suddenly turn a page and read some equivalent of,

But little did he (she) know, that there was

Rather, narrative writers, at their best, are attempting instinctively to recreate the conditions through which all of us, as sentient beings, experience the world: one moment at a time, with puzzlement and confusion in abundance. True, there were twists and turns in our best-laid paths, but most often, when we look back on the information we had, we should have seen those "surprises" coming if we had been paying full attention, and had not been distracted by the so-called details of "daily life."

In other words, storytelling in general connects with us so intimately because it's a mirror image of our personal adventures/misadventures put into—however different in geography, class, gender, etc.—an emotional context with which we can identify.

And storytelling, unlike factual writing, often leaves a

number of unanswered questions, including a desire to confront the storyteller up close and personal, to demand that he/she resolve the troubling question they left us in their book. Killing a beautiful animal, as an act of God? It doesn't make logical sense. It leaves us wondering. What does it all mean in the end? In some of the best narrative work, the reader ends up with more questions to ask than have been answered. Same for the author.

The late novelist and writing teacher John Gardner, in his book *The Art of Fiction*, says that the chief quality of narrative writing is "profluence," and he clarifies the distinction in this way:

> A story contains profluence, and the conventional kind of profluence—though other kinds are possible—in a causally related sequence of events. This is the root interest of all conventional narrative. Because the reader is intellectually and emotionally involved—that is, interested—the reader is led by successive, seemingly inevitable steps, with no false steps, and no necessary steps missing, from an unstable initial situation to its relatively stable outcome.

⤙⫷◉⫸⤚

When Gardner says that "other kinds" [of profluence] are possible, he says a mouthful. Anytime a principle of writing becomes defined or sacrosanct, someone comes along to challenge it—either consciously or subconsciously—and often with memorable results.

Take the principle of saving the ending till last, for example. Truman Capote begins his frequently anthologized short story "Children on Their Birthdays," in this way:

> Yesterday afternoon the six-o'clock bus ran over Miss Bobbit. I'm not sure what there is to be said about it; after all, she was only ten years old, still I know no one of us in this town will forget her.

Likewise, Carson McCullers begins her memorable novella *The Ballad of the Sad Cafe* at her story's end—i.e., the small town in its latter-day form:

> The town itself is dreary; not much is there except the cotton mill, the two-room houses where the workers live, a few peach trees, a church with two colored windows, and a miserable main street only a hundred yards long. On Saturdays the tenants from the nearby farms come in for a day of talk and trade. Otherwise the town is lonesome, sad, and like a place that is far off and estranged from all other places in the world...

By page 2 of the novella, though, McCullers describes a large and mysterious building near the middle of the town, and transitions effortlessly to:

The place was not always a cafe. Miss Amelia inherited the building from her father, and...

And.

And, the narrative begins. What this tells us as writers, I think, is that while an organic and unsuspecting chronology is what most often distinguishes narrative from exposition, a gifted writer of narrative can juggle the *order* of that chronology to match his/her story and purposes to the extent that his/her gift and intuition allows, and still make the work a page-turner.

Sometimes, in the right narrative hands, *what* happens in a story can take an emotional back seat to *how* it happens, as Capote and McCullers and countless other storytellers prove. The secret is the step-by-step unfolding of actual human lives, with all their givens and uncertainties intact.

As William Faulkner once said, "The secret of telling a story is to start with, 'A man went to buy a dog.' But so many different things happen to him along the way that, at the end of the story, when he *does* finally buy a dog, the reader feels a sense of surprise."

Though a successful story can start at the end, the beginning, or anywhere in between, Greek dramatists maintained that in general the most fruitful dramatic possibilities come from beginning a story in the middle. Hence, their principle of starting *in medias res*, or "in the middle of the action."

By the middle of most stories, the characters are already experiencing problems, complications, and conflicts as a result of their earlier behavior and decisions. This is the point at which you're most likely to engage a reader's attention. The events that have gone beforehand—known to editors and scriptwriters as "backstory"—are then worked into the narrative where appropriate, a bit at a time, as the action of the present proceeds toward the climax and conclusion.

Perhaps the most common temptation of a beginning narrative writer is to supply the reader with too much factual information up front—and to supply that information either through authorial commentary or through the character's internal thoughts, rather than letting it unfold naturally through *scene* and *dialogue*, as our personal stories do in real life.

This is partly a matter of a reader's craving for suspense, and partly the fact that one of the joys of reading—and in fact, of living—is coming blindly into the middle of new situations and conversations and using our experience, intuition, and knowledge of human behavior to figure out how these people are related to one another, what has just happened before we arrived, and what is likely to happen next.

When a writer tries to do too much of this work for us, we get irritated because the story begins to seem contrived and pedantic:

As Elena's train neared her hometown, she was already

dreading the inevitable conversation she was almost certain she must have with her mother and father, in which they would officially declare to her that they were divorcing. She had gotten hints of the situation for months now, in letters and phone conversations, but could never quite pin either of her parents down to the whys and wherefores.

As apprehensive as she was, seeing again the familiar old buildings of the city's skyline, she was struck by how different was her sense of impending loss now, than the time— almost exactly five years ago now—when she had faced her own divorce. She and Chad (of whom her mother clearly disapproved, from the beginning) had been together for five years, almost to the day, and she was finally to the point where she could take inventory of her life and almost smile at the bitter symmetry of it: five years as part of a couple, five years alone.

The reason this type of approach makes for unsatisfying reading is that the narrative consists almost entirely of backstory: there's no scene, no dialogue, no description, no action (unless you count the movement of the train), and only the barest hint of a setting. While it gives us a lot of facts about what Elena is going through emotionally, it doesn't allow us whatsoever to vicariously *experience*, through all our senses, her singular life and times, which is undoubtedly the greatest miracle, and the greatest pleasure, that a narrative can afford a reader.

Consider how much more effective and interesting this

story might have been if it had begun with Elena striking up a conversation with a colorful and eccentric stranger, say, an elderly bohemian-looking lady who reminded her, in some ways, of her ex mother-in-law. Or if the story had opened with an arguing couple making a minor scene on the train, and Elena torn between trying to intervene or just feeling silently embarrassment for them.

The possibilities are endless. But the best solutions almost always consist of *scenes:* action, description, dialogue, or all of the above.

Here's the opening of an article I was assigned by a university medical magazine, about people who have survived life-threatening traumatic injuries:

Heights were no problem for James Horne. As a painter on a commercial construction crew, the twenty-seven-year-old Montgomery man's work days often started as this one did: latching his nylon body harness onto a cable, and rappelling off the top of a new six-story parking deck to spray-paint the concrete sides.

He hadn't been working long when the foreman whistled down and told him to come back up top and take a short break: the cable winch had to be moved so a large truck could get past. Afterward, when Horne re-harnessed and went down the wall again, what he didn't realize was that a crucial safety ring on the winch somehow failed to get fastened.

He lowered himself back into place, and was in the

process of swinging sideways to reach a new part of the wall when the cable suddenly went slack and he was surrounded only by air.

"A woman from the office building was standing on one of the middle levels of the deck," Horne remembers now, from his room in a Birmingham rehabilitation center. "And as I fell past her, we locked eyes for just an instant. I've never seen anybody's face so terrified. For that fraction of a second, I had the weirdest sensation that she was the one falling, because she was so scared.

"I think that moment, of seeing her face, will be with me as long as I live."

The difference? Action, description, and dialogue. *In medias res.*

Which is not to suggest that there's some type of formula that can guarantee effective narrative writing. Seasoned writers know that whatever exact strategy worked for them last time will probably not work this time, because every story is a one-of-a-kind jigsaw puzzle made up of different pieces, which must be assembled and reassembled by sheer trial, error, and instinct until it somehow "works" or "hangs together."

As one of my writing professors, novelist Jesse Hill Ford, used to say, "Expositional writing has rules. It can be learned. But *narrative* writing is something you can only try doing again, and again, and again, until you finally *catch on* to it, much like riding a bicycle."

One excellent way to "catch on" to the inner workings of narrative is to take a short piece of writing that you enjoy and admire, and read it again and again and again, underlining and making notes if necessary, until you're able to see beyond its surface effects and down into its bones, arteries, and ligaments.

For my money, one of the most effective and vital openings to a recent American novel is the first chapter of *Fay*, by the aforementioned writer Larry Brown. A participant in my book discussion group said about Brown's novel, "The story unfolds so naturally, it's almost as if the book is reading itself to you." High praise, indeed. And I concur.

(*But*...since all readers and writers are different, if Brown's first chapter doesn't particularly appeal to you, feel free to substitute a story, chapter, or narrative essay by any writer of your choice, as long as (a) it's a piece of writing that excites, involves, and emotionally moves you, and (b) that the person who wrote it is one of your literary heroes, whose name you would someday be proud to have your own writing mentioned in the same breath with.)

Assuming you've chosen the Larry Brown model, try this:

Read the opening scene of *Fay*. It's only seven pages long, and it draws us in with these three paragraphs:

> She came down out of the hills that were growing black with night, and in the dusty road her feet found small broken stones that made her wince. Alone for the first time

in the world and full dark coming quickly. House lights winked through the trees as she walked and swung her purse from her hand. She could hear cars passing down the asphalt but she was still a long way from that.

More than once she stopped and looked back up into the ridges that stood behind her, thinking things over, but each time she shook her head and went on.

South seemed best. She had vague ideas about a coast. She knew it would be warmer in the winter and that one thing drove her in that direction more than anything else. She imagined groves of citrus trees and sunny days picking the fruit and a tiny house where she would have her own groceries and watch television whenever she wanted to. She imagined one solid place where she could stay and maybe she could somehow send for the others then. Or ride a bicycle up and down the flat land with the water always shining out there beyond the shore and birds soaring like in the pictures she had seen of places like that. She kept her head down as she walked and she listened to the night things that called in the ditches and out past the stands of cane and in the clumps of trees that rose from the river bottom.

Put the scene aside for a day or so, then read it carefully once more. Now make a photocopy of the chapter, and put the book back on the shelf—because this time, in the service of learning, you're going to do some serious defacing of the text.

Stop by your favorite office supply store and invest in a pack of highlighter markers of several assorted colors. Bring them home. Take the photocopied pages of the chapter and spread them in sequence across a desk, table, or floor. (Or, you could use photocopies enlarged to 11 x 17 inches and tape them on a wall for easier handling.)

Use a blank sheet of paper or cardstock to make a color-key guide to your highlighters. Mark a big square or circle of each color, and then write beside it what component of a narrative you want that color to represent. Note: This is not an exact science, by any means.

For the sake of argument, let's say that your markers are green, pink, yellow, blue, and orange.

Let's say that your narrative components are "description of action, objects, or settings," (green); "spoken dialogue," (pink); "character's inner thoughts," (yellow); "exposition/back-story," (blue); and "comments by the narrator/author," (orange).

(Note: Since narrative is by nature so subjective, feel free to devise your own categories if different ones work better for you.)

Now, go through the opening scene of *Fay* and use the markers to highlight each sentence, or portion of a sentence, according to the category in which it most closely belongs. If you find this prospect a fearsome task, consider adopting these three ground rules: (1) give yourself no bonus points for neatness, speed, and/or exactitude, unless you are hopelessly obsessive-compulsive; in which case (2) reflect briefly on the role that your obsessive-compulsive disorder plays in your desire to write in the first place, and (3) get over it, at least for the next half-day or so. Nobody need ever see the results of this exercise but yourself. If you won't show me yours, I promise not to show you mine.

Ready?

The first sentence is a fairly straightforward one:

> She came down out of the hills that were growing black with night, and in the dusty road her feet found small broken stones that made her wince.

Clearly a "description of action, objects, or settings," right? We mark it green, and move triumphantly on to the next.

> Alone for the first time in the world and full dark coming quickly.

Hmmm. This one's a bit trickier. Are these the inner thoughts of the character, or a comment by the author? Could be either. And isn't the phrase "alone for the first time in the world" an example of exposition/backstory that's given to help us put the scene in context? Take your best stab, or else hedge your bets by making squiggly lines with two (or even more) different colors. Feel free to split parts of the same sentence into different categories.

If you persevere to the end, you'll begin to understand

intuitively one of the most important characteristics of the narrative form. Namely, what appears upon a first reading to be a seamless flow of words is actually a complex and fragmentary crazy-quilt of images and ideas that only *appears* seamless because of (a) the *sequence* in which the writer chooses to put them, and (b) the effectiveness of any *transitions* (See Chapter One) in seamlessly gluing the loose ends together.

Unlike the expositional style, or the inverted pyramid style, in a narrative, *sequence* (or as John Gardner would say, "profluence") *is everything*. A story stands or falls on the "rightness" of its sequence—even though the concept of "right" allows for infinite variations. And if you can determine, during a careful re-read and re-write, exactly where a sequence falters, presto—you can fix it.

The better and "tighter" your writing is, the greater the chance that fixing something sets off a sort of ripple effect—making it necessary to fine-tune what comes before or after the part you just altered, as well. It's this continual painstaking attention to detail (in the *re-write* stage, not in the writing) that makes possible a story that seems almost to "read itself," the literary equivalent of a burnished piece of fine wood-furniture after hours of planing and sanding, and buffing.

As you come to feel more comfortable reading other author's stories analytically, taking note of these shifting categories and why certain choices are made and not others, you'll be absorbing by osmosis—particularly if you set aside an inviolable time slot each day (even if it's only thirty minutes) to practice your own narrative writing—the skills you need, and which you admire in the writing of others.

Just keep getting back on the "bicycle," and one day you'll feel it straighten up and fly. That's when your writing adventure starts in earnest.

5

Sharpening Your Focus: Choosing and Using Point of View

Of all the choices a writer makes in telling a story, probably the most crucial one is known as "point of view." Namely, *who* is doing the talking? And secondly, what are his/her *credentials* for telling the story to us, as opposed to other voices that could have been chosen?

The "credentials" part unspools its answer gradually as we read the narrative. The "who" portion is something the reader wants to get a sense of far more quickly. We don't need the person's whole life history and resumé up front, much less an elaborate physical description, but we *do* need a general idea of where they stand in regard to the action that's about to unfold—and it's not unreasonable for a reader to expect this general information in the first page or two.

One contemporary writer who's a master at this type of introduction is Richard Ford. Consider this first paragraph of his short story, "Rock Springs":

Edna and I had started down from Kalispell, heading

for Tampa-St. Pete where I still had some friends from the old glory days who wouldn't turn me in to the police. I had managed to scrape with the law in Kalispell over several bad checks—which is a prison crime in Montana. And I knew Edna was already looking at her cards and thinking about a move, since it wasn't the first time I'd been in law scrapes in my life. She herself had already had her own troubles, losing her kids and keeping her ex-husband, Danny, from breaking in her house and stealing her things while she was at work, which was really why I had moved in in the first place, that and needing to give my little daughter, Cheryl, a better shake in things...

Ford doesn't hem and haw over a polite beginning; he jumps into the story with both feet and takes us with him. Notice how much information those few sentences relay to us, in an easy, conversational tone of voice, without seeming stilted or contrived. We know who's telling the story, we know that it will be told in first person (*Edna and I had started down...*), and we know the main characters' basic family situations. The one missing piece is the viewpoint character's name, which we find out in a very natural way on Page 2 when the oil warning light flashes on the car's dashboard and Edna says to him:

"What's that light mean, Earl?"

We, the readers, have everything we need in order to settle back and watch the story happen through Earl's eyes. Just before the oil light goes on, Earl drops the offhand piece of information that the car they're riding in is one he's stolen. Ford could have put this fact in the first paragraph, but he skillfully withholds such revelations and strings them out through the story to keep us in suspense and involved, wondering what other shoe might drop next. The trick is in telling *enough* up front to get us grounded in the character's reality, but not so much that it spoils the story.

Because this implied contract between writer and reader is so important, it's not surprising that poorly chosen or inconsistent point of view is a very common reason (some editors say *the* most common reason) for excluding a piece of writing from publication.

When it comes to mastering point of view, there's good news and bad news for us as writers. The good news is that there's such a broad and varied range of choices as to who tells our story, whether through the viewpoints of one person or several. The bad news is that once we make that choice, we're obliged to stick with it for the duration— whether that duration is 10 pages or 1,000—if we're to maintain credibility with our readers.

Before we look at how to do that, let's get one small piece of technical business out of the way. Because the phrase "point of view" has connotations other than as a writing tool (We might ask someone, for instance, "What's your point of view on the death penalty?"), I've found the substitute term "focus" to be helpful in preventing confusion between a narrative skill and an ideological position. Whatever you choose to call it, the key to effective writing is *consistency of focus* throughout the entire telling.

Now, let's look at our big, tempting barrel of choices. For starters, there's the *omniscient* point of view. In other words, the narrator—who might well be God, for all we know—sees all, knows all, and tells all, and the reader is beneficiary of this vast body of knowledge.

As a result, omniscient focus seems at first blush to be an offer that's hard to refuse, right? After all, don't you want your reader to get the *whole* story? The biggest possible picture? This argument is so convincing that, up until the last hundred years or so, omniscient point of view was a favorite choice of novelists:

The story you're about to hear, dear reader, is a tragedy that wrenches the very heart, and from which you will learn the following lessons...

The downside of telling a story omnisciently is that what readers—especially, readers today—want from a story is suspense, surprises, revelations, and an eventual resolution, all of it through the gradual unfolding of information about the circumstances and characters involved.

Clearly, this is not in a god's job description. If you're omniscient, you know every facet of the story going in, even the ending.

So how do we cut a down a story to human size? By laying aside our omniscient hat and using what's called a *limited* point of view—limited, meaning that the entire story is experienced through the perceptions, thoughts, and actions of an individual character. The focus of this telling is that character's individual consciousness.

Can't a story have *multiple* points of view? Sure it can—though in practice, multiple viewpoint is much easier to pull off in the roominess of a book-length narrative than in an article, essay, or short story.

But this is the clincher: even when you tell a story through multiple characters, the story still must be told through the individual consciousness of *one character at a time*, and with zero cheating on the author's part. Change viewpoints arbitrarily, or too frequently, and the reader gets the equivalent of motion sickness: who's telling this part of the story, anyway? Make up your mind, author, and settle down.

For our purposes, the major no-no is switching consciousnesses in the middle of the stream—or in our case, the middle of the *scene*. As in:

> The first thing Jonathan did after checking his father into the nursing home that morning was to go back to the old house, now empty except for his dad's ancient schnauzer, Benny, and take the dog for a walk. Walking Benny in the familiar neighborhood—which in Jonathan's day had been a whirl of busy families, but was now occupied almost exclusively by elderly widows and widowers—seemed to Jonathan to add at least a touch of normalcy and routine to his Monday, which until that point had seemed totally surreal.
>
> Two blocks up the hill, Benny—who had long been

too old and slow to require a leash—wandered off the sidewalk into the corner of a lush, shady garden and relieved himself (doubly so, in fact) onto a square of lawn so pristine as to have done a golf course proud.

Benny was almost through with this task when Jonathan caught sight, back in the deep shade, of a tiny old woman in a flowered dress and astonishingly wide-brimmed hat of white straw. Shaded though her face was, the stare she gave him in return seemed to him like twin laser beams. And not happy beams, either.

But it wasn't anger that caused her stern expression, just the surprise of being jolted out of her reverie and trying to focus on the glaring patch of sunlight. *That looks like Thomas's oldest boy,* Mrs. Patterson thought. *He lives five hundred miles away! I hope Thomas isn't sick...?*

Whoa, whoa. Technical foul, big time. Give the reader two free throws, and give yourself a slap on the wrist. You've just violated point of view in the worst way.

The story—this part of it, at least—is *Jonathan's* to tell. What's more, here's the very first complication in the young narrative. Namely, Jonathan is already worn out from an emotional morning at the nursing home, and now he thinks he's about to get chewed out by a persnickety old lady for defiling her garden. Hooray! Dramatic tension! That's why it's a very bad move for the author to suddenly *drain* all the tension from the scene by leaping into the thoughts of the tiny old lady in the white hat. (And if the author went on and made us suddenly privy, pardon the expression, to Benny's thoughts on why he chose this particular lawn for his business, we *know* we're in trouble.)

True, Mrs. Patterson may play a significant role in the story to come. She might even play such a significant role that she becomes a viewpoint character herself. But trust me, this is not the time or the place for that metamorphosis.

In a multiple-viewpoint novel or work of narrative non-fiction, the typical place for changing character point of view is *between* sections or chapters. Many writers have made wonderful use of this convention, including British author Julian Barnes in his novel *Talking It Over*, which alternates chapters between the protagonists—two males, one female—involved in a love triangle. Hearing different versions of the same scene (a "he said," "she said" approach) has great potential for irony, comedy, and insight into the vagaries of human nature and the sexes, and shows us that a large part of human behavior is the impulse to justify our own actions over those of others.

But it's important that such a convention be established *as early as possible* in the story, so that the reader knows "the rules." To conveniently introduce a new viewpoint character at the end of a book in order to describe something the main character isn't in a position to see is a clumsy solution, and your reader—even one untutored in the fine points of narrative technique—is likely to realize this sloppy move at some level, and hold it against the book's integrity and credibility.

Now, back to the story of Jonathan and Mrs. Patterson. What *should* the writer of the narrative have done to keep its focus consistent? There are any number of ways. Here's one:

> . . . Shaded though her face was, the stare she gave him in return seemed to him like twin laser beams. And not happy beams, either.
>
> "Uh…hello, there!" Jonathan shouted toward her, in what seemed to him, under the circumstances, an excess of cheeriness on his part. He bent down in a vain attempt to nudge Benny back from the plush grass onto the sidewalk; the dog yelped at him and stood firm until the deed was done to his own satisfaction, which seemed to Jonathan to take forever.
>
> The woman's angry stare continued unabated.
>
> Jonathan had the words in his mouth to say, "I didn't see you sitting there," but decided that wasn't quite appropriate, either. She hadn't budged from her little garden-chair throne in the shade.
>
> "I'm *very* sorry," he said, finally. "I'll take him home and come straight back and clean up, okay?" He wrestled Benny up into arms, with no little difficulty.
>
> She gave no sign of having heard him, or at least not of comprehending. Was she deaf, he wondered? Or was she like his father, confined to a different universe each day depending on the whim of his brain cells?
>
> Before Jonathan had a chance to elucidate on his apology, the woman summarily stood up and marched,

with what looked like balance and vigor, to her back screen door and disappeared inside the house.

Now, what? we wonder, along with our protagonist, Jonathan. Is the woman angry? Is she afraid? Is she going to call the cops? Is she deaf, and going inside to get her hearing aid? Is she out of touch with reality? Is she about to phone his dad's house, and tell him some suspicious character has stolen his dog?

The answer could be any, all, or none of the above. The one thing we *do* know is that our mind races along with Jonathan's own uncertainty, and we begin subconsciously to form the bond a reader forms with a character who's in an uncomfortable position wondering, *Now what?*

The reason we feel empathy and kinship is that such characters are mirrors of ourselves—because we spend so much of our own daily life in uncomfortable positions wondering, *Now what?* We know instinctively that the situation won't be resolved immediately, that Jonathan (and Mrs. Patterson, and Benny, and Jonathan's father) are already moving onward to other challenges and questions. We follow the story to find out what happens.

Besides such major gaffes as switching abruptly from one character's brain to another in order to bring out new information, there's a different type of mistake in focus that, while not as drastic, we should nonetheless avoid for the sake of consistency.

This type of slip-up happens in a passage like this one:

One part of summer vacation Robbie loved most was watching the sun come up over his grandfather's pier. He awoke before daylight without needing an alarm, hurriedly put on his clothes, grabbed the biscuit spread with honey his grandmother had put out for him the night before, and ran the quarter mile downhill to the water's edge.

Once he was in place to see the sunrise, the rest of the day could unfold however it wanted to. This morning, gulls settled lazily onto the pilings as Robbie sat in the sand looking east toward the slowly brightening sky. Finally the edge of the brilliant orange sun surfaced above the water, deepening the color in his already rosy cheeks and glistening off his long black eyelashes. Robbie stood and . . .

Wait. Stop. Time out. We sense a glitch in focus, here. What exactly went wrong?

Just when the writer has us sailing comfortably along inside our character's head (what's technically known as *third person, limited* point of view) on a summer morning, the "camera" is essentially yanked away from Robbie and abruptly spun 180 degrees around, describing his appearance from the viewpoint of another person entirely, even though nobody's on the beach except the kid and the seagulls.

The author has suffered what might be termed an "omniscience hiccup," jumping from one point of view to another, with zero preparation of the reader, in order to squeeze in some information he/she feels we need to know, i.e., what Robbie's face looks like at the moment.

This jump violates the rules because, prior to this point, we've seen everything through Robbie's eyes alone. And obviously, Robbie *can't* see his own cheeks and eyelashes, right? For that, he'd need a mirror. Or at least, a reflecting pool. Or . . .

Ah-*hah*! That's it. What if the tide has just gone out, and there are several small tide pools left in the sand? It would be a cinch for Robbie to lean casually over one of them, and describe the reflection of his sweet little face to our heart's content! Sure . . .

No. Please, don't. Have pity on your poor readers.

Anyone who's done much reading at all will immediately recognize the reflecting-surface ploy as the oldest, and most cobwebbed, trick in the book. (So to speak.) As with any narrative device, this one was no doubt very hot stuff when first invented, but over the years has been so overused as a cheap shortcut around the inherent limitations of third-person point of view that contemporary readers—and especially editors, who read more stuff in a day's time than even the most avid reader—are likely to greet it with a groan and a roll of their eyes.

The *reason* the reflecting-surface technique has been overused to the point of cliché is the notion, particularly among beginning writers, that each character in a story deserves a full-blown physical description (hair color, eye color, type of build, style of dress, the works) as soon as possible after being introduced—and with the narrator at the very top of the descriptive pecking order because, by definition, he/she is always the first character to *be* introduced.

This is not the case.

If the *voices*, the *setting*, and the *action* of a story are convincing enough, the reader can go for very long stretches—sometimes, forever—without requiring a description of each character that's exhaustive enough to pick him/her out of a police lineup.

"But . . ." (you, as a perceptive reader of *A Writer's Tool Kit*, might well respond at this juncture) "aren't we soon to agree, over in Chapter 6, that descriptions in good writing should be as *specific* and *concrete* as possible, without relying on generalities and vague abstractions?"

Excellent point, Perceptive Reader. But for reasons I don't pretend to understand, *physical descriptions* are at least a partial exception to that general principle. A useful rule of thumb in writing is that, all other things equal, the *tone* and *pacing* of a narrative take precedence over other considerations. Any element that draws attention to itself or feels the least bit awkward should be cut from succeeding drafts, no matter our "logical" arguments for including it. In other words, don't shy away from physical descriptions when they seem useful or natural, but don't feel obliged to shoehorn them in.

Take Richard Ford's powerful short story, "Rock Springs,"

for instance. I admired it so much when I first discovered it that I reread it three times in as many weeks, just to savor the details. The characters of Earl and Edna and Cheryl were so real to me I felt I knew them personally, that I might actually see them on the highway sometime and recognize them.

I went back to "Rock Springs" while writing this chapter—several years after first reading the story—with plans to use Ford as an example of how to give physical descriptions of characters in a very brief and yet highly effective way.

What did I find? You guessed it. There aren't any physical descriptions. Zip. Nada.

Nowhere are we told that any of the three people are tall or short, thin or chubby, have straight or curly hair, or eyes of a certain color, or a prominent chin, or a birthmark, or whatever.

How can this be? I can only guess that Ford has rendered their voices, their actions, and the physical details of their *world* so convincingly that my imagination subconsciously supplied the rest.

This may be why serious readers tend to have mixed emotions when they hear that one of their favorite books is to be made into a movie. True, the author's story will gain a wider audience, but the actors will also give each character a permanent and literal face, voice, and mannerisms—which almost never jibe with the very personal ones our individual imaginations envisioned when reading the story on the page.

There's another point-of-view category that bears mentioning, one that falls somewhere between the *omniscient* and *limited* techniques. Jesse Hill Ford gave it the name "panoramic" point of view—and I think it's appropriate that he chose a term with connotations of filmmaking.

If an omniscient scene is told from a bird's eye view, with a godlike narrator following the characters' actions like pieces on a chessboard, and a limited scene is told through the eyes of a particular character, then a panoramic scene most resembles the Hollywood technique of a camera gliding horizontally through the crowd at, say, a mob scene or a social gala—picking up fragments of one conversation and then quickly moving on to another, giving an overall impressionistic sense of the event without lingering for long on one group or character.

Panoramic point of view is a technique you don't see every day (partly, I imagine, because it's so doggoned hard to pull off well), but it can be so effective in certain situations that it bears close study.

Perhaps two of the greatest masters of this unwieldy tool are the Russian author Leo Tolstoy, who uses it to great advantage in the opening ballroom scene of his classic novel *War and Peace*, and Italian novelist Giuseppe Tomasi di Lampedusa, who employs the technique in his 1951 work *The Leopard*. Based on the nationalist revolutionary Giuseppe Garibaldi's conquest of Italy in 1861, di Lampedusa's novel is, to my mind, one of the most underappreciated gems of twentieth-century fiction.

Throughout the ages, many writers have experimented

with variations of all the above techniques—including the so-called "new fiction" or "metafiction" of the 1960s and 70s—with varying results.

(William Faulkner, when asked his opinion of "experimental writing," answered, "All writing is experimental. But they only call it that when the experiment didn't work.")

Are there effective ways of handling point of view in fiction other than the ones we've examined above? Definitely. Any original breakthrough in style and technique involves a writer recombining old elements of the human story (or what Faulkner himself called "the heart in conflict with itself") in new ways. You can do anything you want on a page, as long as you can *make it work* for the reader.

But don't let yourself be put off by the fact that you'll find severe lapses in point of view not only in published works of fiction, but (gasp) even in bestsellers. That doesn't change the importance of playing by the rules, and of treating your readers fairly by never underestimating their intelligence.

Only a handful of writers have it in their power to create works as timeless and eloquent as a William Shakespeare, or a Leo Tolstoy, or a Dylan Thomas. But *all* of us have it in our power not to let sloppiness or laziness keep our writing from being the best it can possibly be.

⟶⟩═◉═⟨⟵

Before we move on to other related matters, here are a couple of suggestions for keeping a consistent point of view while you write:

—If you have a tendency to hop here and there while telling a story within limited point of view, try imagining, as you write, that you are literally *inside* that particular character's mind and body for the duration of the story or chapter and can't get out. You see what they see, hear what they hear, feel the textures their skin touches, etc. You are describing the "movie" that happens as this character's life unfolds: there's only one camera (one at a time, at least), and you're it.

—That said, there's a temptation to get hung up on the *visual* aspect of recording a character's individual focus, or point of view, to the exclusion of other equally important elements that make up our perception. Earlier, we highlighted *voice*, *setting*, and *action* as the three main elements that distinguish one character's point of view from another.

Don't skimp on the voice and the action. If a character is only the reader's surrogate video camera in a particular situation, merely relating what he/she observes, then we haven't brought that character fully to life. In narrative, as in reality, what we *say* and *do* is far more important and interesting, in the long run, than what we *see* and *think*. It takes all the pieces to complete the puzzle. Through intuition and much practice, we learn to supply the needed piece at any given moment.

I'll never forget the evening that one of my beginning efforts at fiction was critiqued in a writing workshop. Turns out, I had made the common mistake I just described, of letting a character do more *seeing* than *doing*. When I finished reading aloud my seemingly endless passage about a man whose "gaze fell upon…" this, that, and the other, and who "surveyed the landscape for…" et cetera, et cetera, and whose eyes at last "touched longingly on…" more of the same, there was a brief silence.

Then one of the workshop participants said with a grin, "That guy in your story deserves a bottle of eyedrops."

Touché.

Now, let's go over just a few more ideas for sharpening the *focus* of your writing that don't directly involve point of view. For the remainder of this chapter it might help to keep in mind, as our goal, the phrase we often hear used to compliment a piece of writing: "It hangs together well."

One part of being true to your material involves not distracting the reader with false leads or expectations, and not going down narrative dead-ends that—while maybe interesting in themselves—have no relevance to the finished product.

Perhaps the best-known dictum that encapsulates this idea is Anton Chekhov's advice to playwrights: don't have a gun hanging on a wall-rack in Act One, unless the gun ends up being fired in Act Three.

That's because readers, whether consciously or not, look for foreshadowing at the beginning of a narrative—clues as to what will happen in the end, or seemingly simple facts that will take on new depth and significance as the story unfolds. It's one of reading's great pleasures, and good writers take pains to lay that foundation well.

Or, as Anne Lamott puts it, in her book *Bird by Bird*:

> Drama is the way of holding the reader's attention. The basic formula for drama is setup, buildup, payoff—just like a joke. The setup tells what the game is. The buildup is where you put in all the moves, the forward motion, where you get all the meat off the turkey. The payoff answers the question, Why are we here anyway? What is it that you've been trying to give?
>
> Drama must move forward and upward, or the seats on which the audience is sitting will become very hard and uncomfortable. So, in fact, will the audience. And eventually the audience will become impatient, disappointed, and unhappy. There must be movement.

We tend to think of the word "drama" in regard to grand spectacle, car chases and explosions, screaming and hand-wringing. But in fact, *every* effective narrative is a drama. Some are big and loud and public, others are small and quiet and intimate. Good stories come in both flavors, as well as an infinite range of forms in between.

Good openings don't just "grab" the reader (as in, "A shot rang out!") but serve to set the stage for the conflict that will be resolved at the end of the piece. One way to do this is with contrasting, or paradoxical, images or ideas.

Unfortunately, "It was the best of times, it was the worst

of times..." is already taken. But there are countless other variations, such as this opening paragraph of Truman Capote's short story, "A Diamond Guitar":

> The nearest town to the prison farm is twenty miles away. Many forests of pine trees stand between the farm and the town, and it is in these forests that the convicts work; they tap for turpentine. The prison itself is in a forest. You will find it there at the end of a red rutted road, barbed wire sprawling like a vine over its walls. Inside, there live one hundred and nine white men, ninety-seven Negroes and one Chinese. There are two sleep houses—great green wooden buildings with tar-paper roofs. The white men occupy one, the Negroes and the Chinese the other. In each sleep house there is one large potbellied stove, but the winters are cold here, and at night with the pines waving frostily and a freezing light falling from the moon, the men, stretched on their iron cots, lie awake and with the fire colors of the stove playing in their eyes.

In a single lyrical paragraph, Capote not only vividly sets the backdrop against which his story will unfold, but manages to create a sense of unease and foreboding as well: the contrast of a beautiful and peaceful natural landscape versus the run-down buildings and the men imprisoned in them, the reflection of the stove fires in their eyes suggesting the intensity of their inwardness, their dreams and fears.

Something, we sense intuitively, is about to happen, to

upset this established, if somber, sense of order. That something is the arrival of a new inmate, an exotic and charismatic
young man from distant shores whose only possession is a
battered guitar inset with rhinestones, which he insists are
diamonds.

The story begins in winter and ends in spring, and by its
conclusion, not only has Capote made dramatic use of every
element in that first paragraph, but the initial image of the
reflected fire in the eyes of the isolated and lonely men take
on a new, expanded, and heartbreakingly plaintive dimen-
sion.

Some anonymous sage of narrative structure has said
that, "There are only two basic story plots: (1) Somebody
gets on the train, and (2) Somebody gets *off* the train."

Obviously there's a bit of exaggeration there, but the
basic idea is a solid one. Some of the most popular and
enduring themes in literature—both in fiction, and in non-
fiction—deal with either (1) a person leaving his or her
familiar surroundings and being forced to deal with a very
different, and potentially threatening, new environment
(think of *Robinson Crusoe*, *Lord of the Flies*, *Alice in Wonder-
land*, *Kon-Tiki*, *The Wizard of Oz*, the powerful contemporary movie *Witness*, and Luke Skywalker of *Star Wars*, for
example), or (2) a community of people in familiar surroundings who suddenly find the natural order of their lives
totally disrupted, for better or worse, by the arrival of a
stranger (or strangers) on the scene.

Capote's story, "A Diamond Guitar," falls into this

second category, as does his landmark work of narrative nonfiction, *In Cold Blood,* Mark Twain's *The Mysterious Stranger,* William Faulkner's *Absalom, Absalom,* the classic Western film *High Noon,* and too many others to mention.

Once your story is up and running, the task that remains is, as farmers of old would say, "to plow a straight row." The good part is, you don't have to do it all at once. You can stop every once in a while, take a look back, see where you're going, and make any necessary adjustments.

In fact, according to author Jesse Hill Ford, that looking back—also known as re-reading what you've already written—is a key component of creating a unified piece of writing.

"It's very important to re-read as you write," Ford said, "so as not to 'drop any stitches.' Instead of starting a new thread out of the blue, see if there's a way to pick up on a thread that's already in the beginning. Your story will be stronger for it.

"That's because the end of a good story is *contained* in the beginning, and it's what gives the story its satisfying sense of inevitability. One rule of thumb I use is that if I find a section to be a particular problem to write, then that section may not be necessary. It may be a hint that I'm off the track, that I'm getting myself into a blind corner.

"That's when it's important to get some distance, take a step back, look at all of the story that's come before, and think about whether there's a better way to proceed."

The concepts of "plowing a straight row" and "not

dropping any stitches" by no means require that an effective
piece of writing be insular, dull, or chronologically straightforward. Thanks to the flexibility given us as writers by the
device of transitions (see Chapter 1) and by a concept known
as "dramatic unities," a narrative can span continents and
galaxies, decades and centuries, and still give a reader the
satisfaction of "hanging together," or being of one piece.

As Ford puts it, "Our early dramatists found that some
things worked on stage better than others, as far as telling a
continuous story to an audience. These basic 'unities' consist
of time, place, and action."

In other words, your narrative can shift across one, or
even two, of these three elements, as long as at least *one*
element remains the same.

An example of the unity of time, for instance, is the
familiar transition, "Meanwhile, back at the ranch . . . ." We
know that the next scene will set us down in a different place
with a different sequence of actions, but as an audience we
don't find that move jarring because the two scenes have
between them the common thread of *time*.

Likewise, in narratives such as the popular film *Same
Time Next Year*, the unifying element is *place*, as we follow
the lives of a couple who carry on an extra-marital affair by
meeting once a year at the same resort hotel. The characters'
moods, lives, and situations change significantly over the
years, but the unity of location makes their story "hang
together."

The same is true of *action*. The common thread of a

similar action can allow a jump to an altogether different time and place without disturbing the narrative fabric. In this paragraph from Kim Wozlenki's novel, *Notes from the Country Club*, for instance, a woman in prison for stabbing to death her abusive husband, Daniel, thinks back on their life together. As the scene begins, the woman is in the prison shower:

> I take my time. The water is reassuring, something that has come from outside the compound. I soap myself slowly, wondering whether it's the shower's privacy or isolation I want more. There are still moments when I wish for Daniel, forgetful moments tinted pink with optimistic nostalgia.
>
> The best kiss we ever shared was in a shower, in a house in Vermont where we were visiting friends. They had gone out in the afternoon, leaving us surrounded by the quiet of deep green woods, and he was there that day. With me and gentle, his fingertips light on the back of my neck . . .

The narrator's giant leap—from a Texas correctional facility to a Vermont forest, and across several years of time—is made credible by the simple common thread of taking a shower.

Once you become familiar with the principle of narrative unities, you'll start seeing them everywhere—even in books and stories you may have read repeatedly, without noticing that the devices were there. That's the whole point. The basic principles of narrative structure have been created and honed by writers over the centuries, by trial and error, to match the ways that we, the audience, most naturally take in information. They're *meant* to be invisible, and the fact that they are is the best testimony that they work.

A final technique that's useful in unifying a story is what author Ford refers to as "tightening"—enhancing and reinforcing the relationships between characters, and strengthening their connection to their place.

As a general rule, the fewer main characters and the fewer settings you have, the more unified the story. With one notable exception: it's hard to hold a reader's interest in a character who is in isolation for long stretches of the narrative, during which we know them only through their thoughts and reflections and not by how they treat other people and vice versa.

Where Westerns are concerned, for instance, this is the reason for the time-tested convention of the "side-kick." Having another personality for the hero to talk and react to, simultaneously "tightens" the story while adding to its dramatic possibilities.

A similar convention, in fiction, is the notion of entrapment. When trouble of any kind starts to happen, our first impulse as human beings is to get out of its way. Audiences instinctively know this, and so they find stories of conflict more credible when the characters involved don't have the option of just getting the heck out of Dodge.

Think about how many memorable stories involve characters thrown together inescapably on an ocean-going ship, airplane, or train, or as adventurers in the middle of nowhere who need one another to survive, as in James Dickey's powerful novel, *Deliverance*, and its resulting film version. Other narrative devices used to keep characters and their conflicts confined to a single area include the familiar bridge washed out by a storm, a community surrounded by flood waters, characters held hostage, an area cordoned off by authorities because of some threat such as an escaped prisoner, and many other variations.

But entrapment doesn't have to be physical, it can be emotional as well. Another way of tightening a story is to intensify the relationships of its main characters. Make them kin to one another, for example, instead of just neighbors or acquaintances. Ties of duty, love, responsibility, honor, and even revenge can be just as entrapping for family members as any force of nature.

In any event, these three strategies—(1) frequent re-reading and considering your options, (2) narrative "tightening," and (3) mastering the principles of dramatic unity—can help immeasurably in making your story everything that it can be.

6

Abstractions: 'All-Purpose' Nouns Are the Bane of Good Writing

They're the bread and butter of the greeting card industry. They're also a chief bane of writers everywhere.

What are they?

Abstractions.

Though they're not technically a part of speech, we know them when we see them—or more accurately, *don't* see them. The first dictionary definition of "abstract" nails the term right on the head:

1. Considered apart from concrete existence: *an abstract concept.*

An exhaustive list of abstractions could fill a book, but these are just a few of the ones we use daily:

Love.

Duty.

Honor.

Truth.

Devotion.

Patience.

Value.

Justice.

Terror.

Meaning.

Outrage.

Faith.

Beauty.

Posterity.

Eternity.

They're all perfectly good, high-sounding, emotionally charged words. For a writer, they present only one problem: close your eyes, and try to picture one.

What do you get?

Let's take *love*. If you're currently deep into a romantic relationship, you might picture the face of your mate. If your children are on your mind, you may picture yourself hugging or holding them, relive the image of bringing them home from the hospital. Likewise, depending on your mood and preoccupations, your mind's eye could conjure up a fiftieth anniversary photo of your parents or grandparents. A volunteer at an animal shelter might picture a particular cat or dog, rescued from the mean streets and nursed back to health by a loving owner.

Or, take *justice*.

A survivor of the Holocaust might envision a dramatic news photograph made during the Nuremberg trials. An attorney or a recent juror might picture a convicted criminal being handcuffed and led off to jail. A student of the civil rights movement may be reminded of a certain memorial to the late Martin Luther King Jr., a black granite wall inscribed with the phrase "Until justice rolls down like water . . .", over which flows an endless sheet of water from a fountain above.

In other words, the possibilities are endless. That's because abstractions are basically "fill-in-the-blank" words. They present no images of their own, but rather offer *associations* that require each reader to call up images from his or her own private grab-bag.

As a result, you'll find that most greeting card verse relies heavily on abstractions: the product is "one size fits all," so one version of a card can be printed by the thousands, their sentiment appropriated by the minds of the giver and the receiver to fit a thousand different circumstances.

> No matter what else may complicate our lives,
> One thing is pure and simple:
> I love you, heart and soul.

It's no accident that this type of writing is called "mushy," because that's literally true. There's no fiber in it, no concrete items of description, no skeleton of a specific time, place, or event in the "real" world. It has as much weight and substance as a brightly colored balloon.

Is there no place for sentiment, then, in good writing? Of

course there is—as long as that sentiment is expressed through concrete images. Take Iowa poet Marvin Bell's poem to his wife:

To Dorothy

You are not beautiful, exactly.
You are beautiful, inexactly.
You let a weed grow by the mulberry
and a mulberry grow by the house.
So close, in the personal quiet
of a windy night, it brushes the wall
and sweeps away the day until we sleep.

A child said it, and it seemed true:
"Things that are lost are all equal."
But it isn't true. If I lost you,
the air wouldn't move, nor the tree grow.
Someone would pull the weed, my flower.
The quiet wouldn't be yours. If I lost you,
I'd have to ask the grass to let me sleep.

For the same reason that abstractions are popular in greeting cards, they're also very much in demand for speeches and sermons. They're accessible and plentiful, they sound inspiring, they don't require a lot of deep analysis by an audience, and they don't pin the speaker down to any specifics—the latter being a special advantage, of course, to candidates for political office, as in this satirical poem by e.e. cummings:

> "next to of course god america i
> love you land of the pilgrims' and so forth oh
> say can you see by the dawn's early my
> country 'tis of centuries come and go
> and are no more what of it we should worry
> in every language even deafanddumb
> thy sons acclaim your glorious name by gorry
> by jingo by gee by gosh by gum
> why talk of beauty what could be more beaut-
> iful than these heroic happy dead
> who rushed like lions to the roaring slaughter
> they did not stop to think they died instead
> then shall the voice of liberty be mute?"
>   He spoke. And drank rapidly a glass of water

Using occasional abstractions may be unavoidable, but if abstractions are at the *center* of your message, then there *is* no message—just a lot of nice sounds and warm-and-fuzzy associations.

The goal and strength of effective writing, by contrast, is *specificity*: creating, or recreating, through language a series of images and scenes that become a recognizable, convincing world of their own—an alternate world for which the reader temporarily puts his or her own expectations and preconceptions on hold, in order to experience it.

How many times have you said, or heard others say, of an especially good piece of writing, "I could just *see* it. I felt as if I were there." That's the highest praise a writer can aspire to. And it's *not* done with clean and cool abstractions, but by getting one's hands dirty with all the complex and untidy elements that make up a day in our sensory lives: the look, the sound, the smell, the taste, and the touch that distinguish a particular experience from all others.

The eccentric poet Ezra Pound made a lot of proclamations in his time, some more sensible and accessible than others, but one that has well stood the test of time is his notion that, "Fundamental accuracy of statement is the sole morality of writing." Indeed, we judge the "truth" of a piece of writing by how accurately it seems to reflect the specific perceptions of the world as we know it—even if that world is a purely imaginary one, consisting of a universe inside a drop of water or an alien civilization a thousand light-years away.

A popular rule of thumb, for example, among writers of fantasy and speculative fiction, is that the more exotic or imagination-stretching the locale of a story is, the more *real* that world's physical details and descriptions should seem, on a sensory level—even if they appear in combinations totally unlike those of our daily lives.

A prime example of the power of specificity in speculative writing is Robert Olen Butler's short story collection *Tabloid Dreams*. The kernel of each story is an outrageous headline, such as we're prone to see in supermarket tabloids:

"Help Me Find My Spaceman Lover," "Jealous Husband Returns in Form of Parrot," "Titanic Victim Speaks Through Waterbed," and more. But Butler is so skillful at investing those concepts with concrete details and an understanding of human nature, within an engaging narrative, that by the end of each piece he's created real-life characters that we love or hate, feel for, jeer at, or cheer for. Within the constraints of their own bizarre worlds, in words, they're just like us.

But perhaps the patron saint of specificity among modern writers is the poet William Carlos Williams, who returns again and again to the concept—directly or indirectly, but always passionately—throughout his considerable body of work. He states his philosophy most directly in his long poem *Paterson*, based on his hometown of Paterson, New Jersey, at one point giving us the memorable line:

"No ideas but in things."

And in what is perhaps Williams's best-known poem, "The Red Wheelbarrow," he comes to the subject in a more indirect way:

So much depends upon
A red wheelbarrow
Glazed in rain water
Beside the white chickens.

Generations of students have been asked to supply their own interpretations of the tiny, unassuming poem, and obviously there are many possibilities. To me, Williams is saying that the entire human experience ("so much depends...") consists of a series of concrete, sensory perceptions through which we think and feel and dream, and on which we base our lives. Though many of those perceptions may seem mundane in isolation ("red wheelbarrow," "glazed in rainwater," "white chickens") they are nonetheless the sole province of real, living human beings and as such should be treasured.

And Williams implies, I believe, that as writers we have as our sole currency, for expressing our ideas and feelings to other human beings, these "mundane" sensory impressions which we must meticulously sort and shape, through our imaginations, until they take on relevance and human meaning.

Even religious prophets and mystics throughout the ages, who have experienced other realities and states of consciousness that are not accessible to the "normal" mind, seem to have considered their transcendental experiences incomplete until they attempted—however imperfect or futile—to reconstruct that experience in concrete, earthly images and metaphors that the rest of us, at some level, can comprehend.

Take a look at Ezekiel's stirring "wheel within a wheel" narrative in the first chapter of the Old Testament book that bears his name. Read the parables with which Jesus taught in the New Testament. Or read the meditations of St. Teresa of Avila in her book *Interior Castles*, or writings by any number of other mystics. Their degree of sensory specificity, despite

their nebulous subjects, is at times breathtaking, even shock-
ing.

The 15th century Sufi poet Kabir, of India, in fact had
the nerve to try putting perhaps the ultimate abstraction, the
concept of "transcendence," into concrete images. He writes,

> The swan has flown to the mountain lake!
> Why bother with ditches and puddles any more?

Likewise, the tradition of Zen poetry has given us centuries' worth of examples of Eastern spiritual philosophies
being translated into real-world terms, such as this untitled
poem from the collection *Dew Drops on a Lotus Leaf*, by Zen
master Ryokan:

> A single path among ten thousand trees,
> A misty valley hidden among a thousand peaks.
> Not yet autumn but already leaves are falling;
> Not much rain but still the rocks grow dark.
> With my basket I hunt for mushrooms;
> With my bucket I draw pure spring water.
> Unless you got lost on purpose
> You would never get this far.

Consider another poem of William Carlos Williams,
written in 1935, one of the most violent eras of the world's
history:

Item

This, with a face
like a mashed blood orange
that suddenly

would get eyes
and look up and scream
War! War!

clutching her
thick, ragged coat
A piece of hat

broken shoes
War! War!
stumbling for dread

at the young men
who with their gun-butts
shove her

sprawling—
a note
at the foot of the page

Williams's fragmentary description of a single atrocity in
some unnamed war is as packed with specifics as a piece of

writing can be ("thick, ragged coat," "piece of hat," "broken shoes," "young men with gun-butts"). And what Williams seems to be saying, by his abrupt shift in tone at the ending, is that as terrifying and degrading as this violent moment is—a horrific example of man's capacity for inhumanity toward his fellow man—it is already in the process of becoming a further, and perhaps equal, degradation. In other words, it will become a footnote, an "item" (i.e., an abstraction) in some book yet to be written.

After wading through "mushy" or abstract writing, coming across a passage of specific details is like a breath of fresh air. Take the opening paragraph of William Goyen's 1950 novel about the fictional small town of Charity, Texas, titled *House of Breath*:

> Oh, Charity! Every frozen morning for awhile in early winter you had a thin little winter moon slung like a slice of a silver Rocky Ford cantaloupe over the sawmill; and then I would go out to the well in the yard and snap off the silver thorns of ice from the pump muzzle and jack up the morning water and stand and look over across the fairy fields at you where you lay like a storybook town, and know that on all the little wooden roofs of houses there was a delicate trail of lacelike rime on the shingles. Then all the chickens and guineas of Charity would be crowing and calling and all the cattle lowing, and the Charity dogs barking (all with a sound that china animals might make if they could crow or call or low), and in that crystal and

moonhaunted moment I would stand, dazzling in the first sunray of morning, and wonder what would ever happen to us all.

We don't know what will happen to them all. But Goyen has made us care, so we read on. In a single paragraph, he's brought to life a town, a time, and a people—and all by the use of the humble, yet powerful, *specific*.

7

Learning Compression: Boiling Down Your Writing to Its Essence

"Brevity is the soul of wit," William Shakespeare assures us. And Samuel Johnson, while acknowledging the merits of John Milton's masterpiece *Paradise Lost*, can't help pointing out that, "None ever wished it longer than it is."

Raymond Carver's best-known advice to writers is, "Get in. Get out. Don't linger. Go on."

Mark Twain once wrote to a friend, "I apologize for this long letter. I didn't have time to write a short one."

It was also Twain who advised, "When you find an adjective, kill it."

But, I could go on about brevity for pages and pages.

The fact is, this chapter is not about brevity *per se*, but a particular subspecies of it that can be a very effective tool for improving your writing: "*retro*-brevity," if you will, a part of the revision process that's also known as *compression*.

Compression is not to be confused with wholesale cutting and shortening, though it involves snippets of both. "Cutting" a piece of writing means deleting the sentences or paragraphs representing facts or ideas that are least important in terms of the finished product, portions that don't carry their weight narratively.

Compression, on the other hand, means maintaining all the ideas that are already there, only doing it in *fewer words*.

Not only does compressing give a piece of writing a more energetic and muscular feel, but the process itself is an ongoing education in the fine points of narrative structure. Think of it as Nautilus exercise for the writer's brain.

Twain's comment about a short piece of writing requiring more time than a longer one, while whimsical, also contains a very large kernel of truth.

One of the hardest and most time-consuming writing assignments I've ever taken on was to create two dozen "cameos," or personal profiles, of people throughout my state who, at some point of crisis, had their lives changed for the better through the outreach efforts of a particular urban university. The layout and design of the publication was already in place, and the space allotted for each profile was (are you ready for this?) 200 words. And maybe, in a rare case or two, as much as 210.

Under normal circumstances, left to my own devices, I can easily spend 200 words describing the view outside the window of the room where I write: namely sky, a neighbor's slate roof, and a couple of big trees. Boiling a dramatic and emotional *life story* down to that length was quite a leap—either of faith, or naiveté. Maybe a little of both.

The average interview for each piece ran about 30 minutes, though a couple of them stretched to 45 minutes and one to a little more than an hour. After that, the task was to read and re-read each set of notes, with pencil in hand, looking for a beginning, a middle, and an end.

This done, I wrote a first draft of each piece—none of them fewer than 250 words, and a couple nearing 300—and set the admittedly pudgy manuscripts aside for a day or so. The reasons for this were twofold. One was to let the pieces become, as some writers put it, "cold." Because you have less of an emotional investment in the language than when you're in the white-heat of constructing a first draft, a cold re-read allows you to see with much greater objectivity which sentences sing and which ones sag.

The other reason is that our subconscious minds are often far more resourceful about writing—particularly in matters of structure and problem-solving—than our most fine-tuned waking intelligence. It's not unusual for our subconscious to keep working on such problems even after we've laid a manuscript aside to concentrate on other pursuits: reading a book, taking a walk, or having a sandwich.

Whoever invented the admonition "Sleep on it" was aware that a good night's sleep is a particularly fertile workplace for the subconscious. Many writers—myself included—make it a point to re-read a problematic scene or chapter late in the evening, then to purposely put the piece of writing out of conscious thought.

Reading a good book on a totally different subject is one popular strategy. Other writers swear by one of a wide range of pursuits including bridge, chess, needlepoint, charcoal drawing, oil painting, or even a computer game.

Then, after a night's sleep, our deeper brain will, surprisingly often, come up with a simple but ingenious solution that leaps over the previous evening's structural deadend and once again gets us moving in the right direction.

Re-reading these too-long profiles with a fresh eye, I was able to see more easily which dead-wood words and sentences weren't pulling their own weight and could be eliminated without loss to the narrative.

One of the pieces, which I finally compressed to its fighting weight of 193 words, read this way:

Norma Brinkley grew up on a small farm in Antioch, Tennessee. But life there was far from idyllic. By seventeen she had a baby daughter and a head start on a drinking problem.

Her introduction to Birmingham wasn't promising, either: registering at a halfway house for recovering alcoholics. But, when the program's vocational testing showed she was college material, she enrolled—a bit skeptically— at UAB.

Now, Norma's working on her graduate degree in psychology. She's renewed an old love, too—writing songs and playing the guitar. Her classmates in the Honors Program encouraged her to enter the annual UAB Follies. She won first place. In the months since, she's sung her songs at several concerts and on local TV. And her daughter, now grown, is planning to enter UAB's medical school.

Someday Norma hopes to sit eye-to-eye with a teenage girl in counseling and give her the advice she needed so badly, herself, twenty years ago. "I'll tell her it's tempting to count yourself out when you stumble and fall down," Norma says. "But you have it in your power to get up and go on.

"I've gotten up. I'm going on."

Along the way, I learned that the scaffolding necessary for a coherent mini-narrative requires surprisingly few components: a beginning, middle, and end; one or more scenes or images; and some brief dialogue.

Another profile, about a student escaping political repression, compressed down to these 188 words:

It was 1988 in India, and Monoj Kaplash was living his long-time dream—attending college, preparing for medical school. But, almost overnight, his country's worsening political and religious strife turned the dream into a nightmare.

A new quota system for universities, based on social class, left him wondering if he'd be allowed to return to school the next year. Even in India, Manoj knew of UAB's reputation in the health sciences. He sent his application and began pondering the idea of going to school in the U.S.

That was before he was awakened in his dormitory one morning with the news that 21 of his classmates had been killed in a clash with police. The tragedy made up his mind for him. Within a few weeks, he was waving good-bye to his family from the window of a plane bound for America.

This quarter he's studying chemistry and biology at UAB and planning a career in nephrology. Some days he's homesick for the village where he grew up. "India is always my home," he says, in careful British-flavored English, "but my future is not there. My future is here."

I also learned that, when push comes to shove, a scene doesn't have to consist of long descriptive passages. Sometimes, it's a matter of word choice: Brinkley's "registering at a halfway house for recovering alcoholics," rather than the more nebulous "living" or "spending time" there. And Kaplash's "waving good-bye to his family from the window of a plane bound for America," as opposed to the generic "flew to the United States."

Not only is compression a valuable educational process, but, as often happens with the mechanics of writing, one good turn has a ripple effect that benefits other areas of the piece as well.

Saving words, for instance, often requires changing a sentence from passive to active voice— "The truck hit her car broadside," for example, rather than "Her car was hit broadside by the truck"—a good habit to get into, even when word length isn't crucial.

Compression also helps you prune out those awkward dependent clauses, trailing clouds of gerunds and prepositions as they come, which seem particularly bundlesome when used to begin a sentence before the subject is even named:

"Walking rapidly down the dark, narrow stairwell with the key tightly in hand, worrying about what the secluded room might contain and fearing that others might already have gotten the word about what was happening, Marian..."

More active sentence construction might render the same scene this way: "Marian hurried down the dark, narrow stairwell, clutching the key to the secluded room. What would she find there? And what if the others had beaten her to it?" Not only do we shave off almost 20 percent of the word count, we also gain clarity and immediacy.

Likewise, for pruning unnecessary modifiers. Mark Twain's admonition, "When you find an adjective, kill it," may be a bit overzealous, but his heart is in the right place. There's nothing wrong with adjectives, *per se*—it's just that they're too often used carelessly by writers as a crutch to prop up a weak or imprecise noun. A "gust" is generally preferable to a "strong wind," for instance, and a "tangle" of hair has more punch and economy than an "unruly mass."

Adverbs and adverbial phrases can be crutches, as well. A person in a narrative who "walks with a casual air" may do better to "stroll" or "saunter." And someone "moving in a rapid manner" could "hurry" or "rush" to better effect. As Twain himself noted, "The difference between the right word and the almost-right word is like the difference between lightning and a lightning bug."

And while we needn't stamp out every adjective and adverb when we revise our manuscript, we do owe it to ourselves to at least look on them with a jaundiced eye and consider whether a different choice might be better.

A caveat, however: it's perfectly fine for a person in a piece of writing to simply "walk" somewhere, or "say" something. And there's nothing wrong with a writer repeating such a word or phrase. If you strive too hard simply for variety's sake—i.e., if your walkers start to "perambulate" and "traverse," or if your talkers suddenly get a yen to "expostulate" and "remonstrate" and "exclaim," your readers will quickly catch you with your thesaurus showing. Words shouldn't stand out for their own sake, but rather do their narrative job with the least amount of fuss and frills.

The phrases "he said" and "she said" can appear numerous times in an extended conversation without troubling a reader—that's because experience has trained us to use these merely as helpful clues to who is saying what. Their purpose served, the attributions tend to recede into the background of what's actually being said.

(Although, humorist Ring Lardner Jr.'s classic bit of dialogue— "'Shut up,' he explained"—has charms all its own.)

As important as compression is, it's also important to know when to quit. Chief of all, a compressing writer would do well to use kid gloves when rewriting people's dialogue.

The natural rhythms of the spoken language can't be faked; don't give in to a temptation to take the life out of a conversational line by making it sound like exposition in order to shave off a few words.

For instance, a person saying "I found out that . . ." so-and-so was the case sounds perfectly natural. Change that phrase to "I determined . . ." in order to save words, and suddenly the sentence doesn't ring true at all—unless the speaker in question is an expert witness testifying in court.

Overall, though, where writing is concerned, brief is better. Punchy is preferable. Succinct is super.

And what if some reader finishes your piece of writing and "wishes it longer than it is"? Congratulations. You've gotten one of the highest compliments a writer can receive.

8

The Big Question:
Which Comes First, Flesh or Bone?

There are as many different approaches to writing as there are writers, but over the years I've found there seems to be a great divide between two main categories.

One type of writer tends to see the "big picture" up front: the entire arc of a storyline envisioned immediately and whole, as if illuminated by a flash of lightning. *Action*. Beginning, middle, end, all there for the taking.

This type of writer tends to work very fast and confidently, with the energy of a freight train on a downhill grade, sometimes finishing the first draft of an entire book in months, or even weeks, keeping long hours and sustaining themselves on caffeine and/or nicotine or both.

One way to recognize a "big-picture" writer is by how they describe the process: "I just have to get down the 'skeleton' of the story first," one of them might say, "and then go back through and flesh it out."

Indeed, if you were to read one of these first drafts—even

from some accomplished and celebrated writers—you might be appalled. The writing can be clumsy, abrupt, incomplete, and disjointed. The characters may seem sketchy, one-dimensional, and occasionally even confused, themselves, by what they're doing in this particular book.

But that's all right, because the "skeleton" draft is nothing like the official version that will magically appear several drafts later, inside glossy book-jackets smelling of fresh ink, on the bestseller shelves of your bookstore.

I've known a few writers like this, over the years. Some are such meticulous organizers of plot and structure that they line the walls of their writing room with butcher paper or pieces of poster board, on which they draw diagrams listing the basic action steps in each chapter; the family trees, motivations, and predispositions of the main characters; and miscellaneous concerns and structural problems that will have to be figured into the mix at some point, as in an enormous, multi-level chess game. Some of these writers use color-coded flags, highlighters, sticky-notes, and pushpins to help lend order to this manageable chaos.

I hate these people.

Er . . . scratch that.

What I mean to say is that I desperately *envy* such writers their clear thinking, their organizational skills, and their instinctive grasp of plot complexities.

That's because I fit into the "other" group, the writers who wouldn't recognize a story's skeleton if it kicked us in our shin with its bony foot.

Therein lies the great divide.

One of my literary heroes—and perhaps the most quotable of all—is Flannery O'Connor. Once upon a time a New York editor, frustrated by how slowly and circuitiously she worked, suggested that Flannery could be far more productive by simply writing a brief *outline* of her story before she began. To which Flannery replied,

"But how can I know what I think till I see what I've said?"

O'Connor, I'm convinced, was not being at all flippant—rather, she was merely expressing with honest spontaneity the plight of all writers whose basic approach (or as skeptics might say, *lack* of approach) is overwhelmingly *intuitive* and *instinctive*, rather than logical and cerebral.

Instead of starting with a story "skeleton" and "fleshing it out," these writers reverse the process. They begin by creating narrative "flesh" —scenes, descriptions, characters, sensory impressions, images, dialogue—as though out of thin air, purely on a "hunch," proceeding as heedlessly and trustingly as someone in the grip of a dream, with no clear idea which direction, if any, the story will eventually take.

After creating—inch by inch, pound by pound—enough of this flesh to fairly judge, the writer puts the manuscript aside, gets some distance, and gives a cold, hard look as to whether it contains the skeleton (or at least, a bone or two) of a viable story before proceeding.

British novelist Alan Sillitoe (probably best known for his novella *The Loneliness of the Long-Distance Runner,* which became a distinguished independent film introducing actor Tom Courtenay) has said that, for him, this point of assessing the viability of a manuscript comes most often at around the 100-typewritten-pages mark.

"By then," Sillitoe says, "I'm usually able to determine whether the story has enough loft to clear the runway."

If a writer finds in the affirmative, the course is clear—full speed ahead, ideally to a completed first draft. Or, more realistically, to another crisis point that John Gardner describes, in his *On Becoming a Novelist*, this way:

"Writing a novel is like heading out over the open sea in a small boat. If you have a plan and a course laid out, that's helpful. If you drift off course, checking the stars can help you find a new course. If you have no map, no course laid out, sooner or later confusion will make you check the stars."

Novelist and journalist Dennis Covington, whose narrative non-fiction book *Salvation on Sand Mountain* was a finalist for the National Book Award, reports a similar phenomenon:

"For me, the really bad 'slough of despond' always comes at around the halfway point of a book. I completely lose my way. It's just like falling into a big dark hole, and it feels like I'm never going to get out. But eventually, I do."

While "logic-driven," or plan-ahead, writers are often known for their erratic hours, flexibility of schedule, and resistance to disruptive influences such as noise (some actually feel more comfortable working in public places, such as a coffee shop or a neighborhood park, saying that the surrounding action seems to stimulate their thoughts), most of the intuitive-type writers I've talked with over the years feel an intimate connection with solitude and the early morning hours, as though their best writing takes place in a semi-dream state from which they fend off the real world as long as possible.

One of the latter is acclaimed horror writer Clive Barker, who's interviewed in Naomi Epel's book, *Writers Dreaming*. Barker tells Epel:

> I spend most of my working day in some kind of dream state. That is to say, I get up from my bed, I shower, drink my coffee and go to my desk, which is literally ten yards from my bed. I then start, on a normal day, a process which will maybe take me eight or ten hours, writing about something that my inner eye is seeing. It's not like I'm getting up in the morning, as most people do, and stepping out onto the street and being slapped into the solid problem of how I get the car to start. Or whether the subway is crowded. Or how the boss is going to feel about me that morning. None of those things intrude.
>
> I live alone. I don't have anyone to wake me from the reverie into which I've woken when I open my eyes. I don't get a double waking, I only get a single one. And, if I'm lucky, I plug back into this kind of—I'm not saying somnambulance—but I do think that if somebody were to secretly photograph me while I was writing, I'd probably look like a lunatic.

By this particular point in this particular chapter, would-be writers are no doubt figuratively waving their hands in the air to ask, "But which of these two diametric approaches toward structure in writing is the *best* one to take?"

To which I would answer that the question is beside the point. Is it best to be born dark or fair, male or female, shy or garrulous, tall or short, stocky or thin? Like our birthright, our basic orientations as writers are for the most part beyond our control. In my own experience, I've never known a writer who successfully transitioned totally from the plot-oriented mode to the intuitive, or vice versa.

The answer, as in real life, comes down to doing the very best you can with whatever attributes you've been blessed/cursed with. Although, there are many accommodations and learning situations in between. An especially tentative or hesitant writer, who claims to wait upon "inspiration" and being "in the mood" might benefit from working as, say, a reporter for a daily newspaper.

It's a major education to find that you can go to the office at 8 a.m., do basic research and preparation to interview at 9 a.m. (a) a visiting total stranger who is (b) an expert on a topic you've never heard of, and (c) nonetheless write a very literate and credible article by noon, which—with some good copy editing—will appear in that evening's same newspaper under your byline. (So much for writer's block.)

The full-speed-ahead, story-above-all contingent, who roll their eyes at this digression, would likewise benefit by having (as is very often the case) their stories and novels chosen to be converted into scripts for plays, or screenplays for movies. At that point, they find the collaborative nature of same—dealing with other professionals who assertively bring their own strengths, weaknesses, and insights to such a group project—to be both educational and tremendously frustrating.

And though "skeleton first" writers are generally noted for their regular and prodigious output, while morning-dreamers tend to work more hesitantly and circuitously, it's not a hard-and-fast rule.

Few popular writers, for instance, are more productive than Stephen King, but he also feels an allegiance toward mornings and the dream state:

"Part of my function as a writer is to dream awake," King has said. "And that usually happens. If I sit down to write in the morning, in the beginning of that writing session and the ending of that session, I'm aware that I'm writing. I'm aware of my surroundings. It's like shallow sleep on both ends, when you go to bed and when you wake up. But in the middle, the world is gone and I'm able to see better."

The world is gone, and I'm able to see better.

This seemingly simple, but all too elusive, action is so vital to a writer's daily work time that there have been entire books written about it.

Six of the very best, I think—and ones which I keep fruitfully returning to, over the years, because they continue to offer new insights upon re-reading—are:

—*Becoming a Writer*, Dorothea Brande

—*Zen and the Art of Writing*, Ray Bradbury

—*Writing Down the Bones: Freeing the Writer Within*, by Natalie Goldberg

—*The Writing Life*, Annie Dillard

—*Bird by Bird: Some Instructions on Writing and Life*, Anne Lamott

—*On Becoming a Novelist*, John Gardner

The last time I checked, all these were not only still in print but available in inexpensive ($10 and under) paperback editions.

And as you might gather from the titles, all the books deal not so much with the technical and stylistic aspects of writing as with the psychology of it: the daily struggle inside each writer's mind to create the most, and best, work possible within the maddening constraints of personal habit, temperament, self-esteem (or more likely, lack thereof), nagging doubts, jealousies and resentments, and such niggling responsibilities as (a) acting human toward your loved ones, and (b) earning a living.

Or, as John Gardner phrases it in his apt introduction to Brande's 1934 (!) work, "The root problems of the writer are personality problems."

Most often, the largest problem is learning to make the best of whichever writing temperament that nature has given us: the bone variety, or the flesh variety.

I boil it down this way: If you're a "bone" person, who

can get a compelling story down on the page—from beginning, to middle, to end, however rough or jagged-edged, and then rewrite as many times as needed to flesh out and refine it—more power to you.

Try not to be intimidated by the fact that many of your fellow writers (*i.e.*, the "flesh" people) will be very envious. You can always spare their feelings a bit by fudging the facts—such as stretching out the length of time it takes you to "get the basic story down," and avoiding such confident declarations as "the idea came to me all in one piece."

Your fleshy counterparts have very good reason to be envious of this skill. The hard facts are that, particularly in today's publishing industry, a writer who can tell a compelling story, even if his or her prose style is not breathtakingly original, is likely to be published much sooner than a writer who can create stunning images and make the language sing but who has trouble staying with a story and not going off on tangents or hitting narrative dead-ends.

Perhaps the most renowned flesh-writer of the past century—and an amazingly successful, beloved, and influential one—was Thomas Wolfe. Neighbors of the young would-be novelist would later recall him writing in seclusion from dawn until dusk, then rewarding himself with a walk downhill to a tavern, from which he came back triumphantly singing to himself, "I wrote ten thousand words today, ta-dah! I wrote ten thousand words today, ta-dah!"

As history (maybe a bit mythologized, but still) has it, when Wolfe went seeking publication of his fiction, his "manuscript" didn't fill an envelope, but rather a large box. This was because he wasn't sure whether his writing was a novel, or two, or more, or a mix of stories and novellas, or . . .

Wolfe was looking for an editor with the expertise to help him sort things out. After many an uneasy rebuff from editors who cast an understandably jaundiced eye at the sheer volume of his output, he was benevolently taken under the wing of an editor named Maxwell Perkins—who also, incidentally, played a major role in the careers of Ernest Hemingway and F. Scott Fitzgerald.

Perkins worked meticulously with Wolfe's huge rough draft until he had trimmed and fashioned it into the novel that was published in 1929, to great acclaim and commercial success: *Look Homeward, Angel*.

But that was then, this is now. Because of sweeping changes in the publishing industry, including mega-mergers and an increasingly competitive economic climate, a hopeful writer is not likely to find an agent or an editor who has the time, wherewithal, or inclination to troll their submissions in search of a diamond in the rough. More than ever, the responsibility is on the writer to ensure that his or her work is as cohesive and polished as it can possibly be before sending a manuscript off into the wide world.

Still, most agents and editors have a wealth of war stories about clueless cover letters they've received over the years: "I don't know if my writing is any good or not, so I'm sending it for your opinion." Or, worse, "I know this is very rough and needs a lot of work, but . . ."

("When you think about it, it's really an insult," one agent told me. "Why should somebody waste my time by sending me a piece of writing that even *they* know is not *finished* yet?")

Of course, every manuscript, after being purchased, goes through varying amounts of fine-tuning during the process of editing and publishing. But the cardinal rule for aspiring writers is that you never submit a manuscript *until it's as good as you can possibly make it. Period.*

The vast majority of writers, not surprisingly, need help in achieving this. Most published writers, when asked, freely give credit either to a workshop teacher or other established author who took an interest in their work and gave them moral support and technical guidance that proved invaluable in their breakthrough to the printed page. One of the best venues for making these kinds of connections is a writers conference, of which thousands, of varying sizes and focuses, are held annually across the U.S.

To find out about these events, call the English departments of colleges and universities in your area. Ask your librarian or bookseller if they know of local writers groups who are accepting new members. Go to a meeting, and ask the folks there for suggestions of workshops or conferences that they've found to be helpful. And, keep an eye out for announcements in such periodicals as *Writer's Digest* and *Poets & Writers*, as well as the Sunday books section of your local newspaper.

Keep in mind, though, that there are *two distinct and separate* types of editorial help that a writer needs: one is called "story editing," the other "line editing."

A story editor, rather than sitting down and meticulously going word-by-word through your manuscript with a blue pencil in hand, approaches your work in the spirit of a typical—ideal—reader. A story editor looks at the forest, not the trees.

Do the events you're writing about flow naturally from one into the next? Does the opening of your story raise questions and expectations that keep the reader turning the pages to find out what happens next? Does the pacing of your narrative match its content? Are there sections that drag, that can be trimmed down and work better? Are there parts that feel rushed, where the reader would prefer to linger a bit more? Does your story make the most of the people who are in it? When those characters take actions and make choices, do the actions and choices and changes of heart reveal the individuals' hopes and fears, rather than seeming arbitrary or preordained? The bottom line: does the "motor" of your narrative run roughly or smoothly? How can the story be made better, in the big picture?

If story editing is a bird's-eye-view, "line editing" is a look through a magnifying glass: at the level of individual words, sentences, and paragraphs, what changes can be made in your work to create a more seamless experience for the reader on a line-by-line basis? Would this long sentence work better as two short ones? Did you realize you repeated the word "somewhat" three times in two pages? Do you fall into the habit of relying on adjectives and adverbs to prop up weak nouns and verbs that could have more punch? Isn't this particular phrase almost a cliche? Couldn't you find something fresher? At one point you say the guy's car is red, and at another you call it "maroon"? Which is it?

Both levels of editing are important to the success of a piece of writing. But because of their very different natures, story editing advice is both (a) harder for the writer to find, and (b) harder to take once you've found it.

The reasons are apparent. Though a good line editor might mark up your manuscript unmercifully with suggested changes, even wipe out entire paragraphs with a single stroke, you can nonetheless sit down to your word processor and make those changes in relatively short order—even with a fairly large manuscript, a matter of a day or two.

A story editor, on the other hand, is apt to drop bombshells that begin with the glorious but frightening phrase, "What if?"

What if the main part of the story was set in the summer, the growing season, and ended with winter coming on, rather than the way it is now? *What if* the main character had a different career—was on the road a lot, say, rather than working out of that small office? *What if* the strange new couple that moves next door was not a couple, but a single woman? And *what if* she arrived before the main characters' wedding, instead of after?

Et cetera.

Regardless of the nature of the *what if*s, the writer's initial response is, understandably, a single thought: *But…if I did that, I'd have to start all over.* It's a despairing, heart-sinking feeling, considering the amount of time and emotional energy you've already expended on this labor of love—and this is true to the tenth power, if the piece of writing is one you had hoped might be your breakthrough into actually being *published.*

At this point, the story editor—if he/she is a seasoned one—will shrug and lighten the mood: "Well, it's just an idea. You know. Give it some thought. We can talk again."

I know this scenario from hard experience. Hard, but thankful. Here's what happened to me . . .

Years ago, even after I had managed to publish dozens of articles and op-ed pieces in newspapers, and a good deal of short fiction in magazines (including *Redbook*), the craft of the novel somehow remained totally impervious to me. I took workshops, read how-to books, dissected great novels for their mechanical technique, and then—while working a full-time office job—scrounged every spare minute of early mornings, weekends, and holidays writing my first novel. In a little more than a year, I had finished a first draft.

I spent the next three months revising and polishing it, several times through, into what I considered a final draft. As I had no idea how to approach a literary agent, I began—with tremendous hope and no small trepidation—to send out a query letter and sample chapters directly to editors at New York publishing houses whose names I had gotten from *Writer's Market.*

Over the next six months or so I received a couple of anonymous, form-letter rejections, then—miracle of miracles—a real letter from a flesh-and-blood editor asking to read the whole manuscript. I complied, my heart racing, fingers and toes crossed.

Several weeks later, the editor replied: it was a rejection, but one contained in a long letter telling me the writing style was "excellent," but that the novel was "in need of a good deal of restructuring." Still, he said, he'd be very interested in reading my next draft of this book, or anything else I wrote in the future.

I was simultaneously high as a kite, devastated, and dumbfounded. To my regret, the action I took next was dictated by the fact that I was (a) Southern, (b) painfully shy, and (c) terrified of appearing ignorant to a real, live editor. If I were good enough to be published, I reasoned, I had to write a novel that wouldn't need "restructuring"—whatever that meant. Close call, but I had struck out. I had to try again.

I wrote the editor a cordial letter thanking him for his encouragement, and telling him that I was hard at work on a new novel (I had started one the next day) which I would send to him when it was finished—and one that, I reassured myself, wouldn't need any doggoned restructuring.

I worked on the second novel a little over a year, revised it for a couple of months—certain that it was better than my first effort—and mailed it off to my benefactor in New York.

Several weeks later, I got a letter from a different editor at the same publishing house. The first editor had changed careers, but his replacement said he liked my writing very much.

Unfortunately, he said, this manuscript had some "structural problems," but that he would welcome the chance to read future versions of it, etc. I mailed the manuscript to different publisher for a second opinion, which I got in a couple of months: it was essentially the same as the first opinion. I tried a third publisher. Ditto.

I sat down and started another novel.

This scenario repeated itself for another six years. By this time I had written five whole novels and a fairly long novella—all widely praised, but none purchased. Daunted but unvanquished, I started writing my seventh book.

That spring, I attended a writing conference at a local college. One of the speakers happened to be a former fiction editor for some large New York houses who had changed careers (he had gone back to school to become a psychotherapist, which I thought very appropriate) and moved to the West Coast.

As he described the daily life of a book editor, I realized with growing wonderment that their talents could mostly be summed up in one word: *Restructuring.*

And when the speaker mentioned that he occasionally did book editing on a freelance basis for individuals, I felt as if his remarks were accompanied by an imaginary heavenly chorus. When he finished his talk, my congenital shyness fell away and I almost sprinted (not knocking anyone over, fortunately) to intercept him at the edge of the stage, introduce myself, and get his business card.

Over the next two years, I mailed him sections of my manuscript as I completed them, and via return mail and some long-distance phone calls he taught me story-editing. It was the best money I've ever spent.

Not that the process was an easy ride. Far from it.

About nine months into the first draft, for instance, the hero of my novel (which would eventually be published as *The Shining Shining Path*) was a lonely, depressed, recently divorced, forty-ish guy who made his living as a traveling salesman of athletic wear for small college sports teams.

One day the editor phoned me. "I've been thinking," he says. "This guy listens to music all the time, in his car. Rock 'n' roll is a big part of his life, right?"

"Right," I said, with no idea where this was heading.

"What if…" the editor said, "he wasn't a salesman, but a concert promoter?"

"Concert promoter," I repeated, fumbling for a response. "You mean, like, nightclubs and stuff?"

"No, no," the editor said. "Concert halls. Stadiums. World tours. The Rolling Stones. The big time. But then something happened, and changed it all."

"Like what?" I asked.

"Hell if I know," he said. "Just thinking out loud. Anyway, you can take it or leave it. But sleep on it. Give it some thought."

My first thought was that this guy needed psychiatric

help. But before bedtime I re-read parts of my manuscript, and thought about what he had said. I slept on it.

The next morning, I woke up feeling as excited as a little kid. A rock promoter! Of course. Think of the possibilities. Why hadn't I thought of this to begin with? Starting almost entirely from scratch, in the pre-dawn hours of the next six months, I wrote like someone possessed.

I mailed him a second batch. It came back with three single-spaced pages of suggestions. Red lines were drawn through one whole chapter of my precious manuscript, and large sections of others. His notations in the margins said things like, *Interesting, but beside the point...* and *When are we going to get back to the STORY?*

One day, after reading his red-inked care package, I used some bad language and threw the manuscript against the wall. That night, I picked it up and read it again. I slept on it. Nine-tenths of the time, his comments ended up making sense—though not right away.

Eventually, the manuscript became a "real" novel. It was "restructured" to within an inch of my life, but it was published. For weeks afterward, I made sporadic visits to libraries and bookstores to see it on their shelves, just to make sure I hadn't imagined it. And now, I can't imagine the story of the book being any other way than the final version. When I come across pieces of early drafts containing characters and scenes now nonexistent, the words seem as foreign as hieroglyphics.

Story editing, in a nutshell. I'm convinced that if I had

sought out a story editor earlier, I could have published ten years sooner than I did.

Am I still a flesh-writer? Sure. I'll always be. But along the way I've internalized enough bone-writer skill to tell a book-length story, too.

Eventually.

9

Doing Dialogue: Bringing Spoken Language to Life on the Page

Dialogue? *That should be easy. You just write down the kind of stuff people say, right?* Well, yes and no.

At one level, we're all experts on dialogue. Not only do we hear it and speak it every day of our lives, we've also learned by hard experience, over a lifetime, that what people *say* and what they *mean* are not always (a cynic would say rarely) one and the same.

As a result, we tend to "filter" the literal words that other people say to us through a series of our own considerations: their tone of voice, their facial expressions, their body language, the particular situation at hand, and when appropriate, what we know through past experience of that person's character and personality.

Likewise, when speaking to another individual, we choose our words to create the specific *impression* we want that person to get from what we're saying—above and beyond the literal facts that the conversation is conveying.

Picture yourself relating the same basic information

about some incident—a traffic accident, a job promotion, adopting a pet—to various audiences. Chances are that your parents or grandparents would be told a somewhat different version than your best friend. A neighbor you meet in the grocery aisle would hear yet another version; a newspaper reporter interviewing you, still another. And so on.

Even when we're not lying or trying to hide anything, we automatically tailor information according to the needs and expectations of the person we're speaking to, and vice versa.

As a writer, tapping into our own innate knowledge of what conversation really is—how fluid, subjective, and fragmented—is one of the most valuable resources we bring to the table in making spoken language "work" on the written page.

At that point, though, dialogue gets a little trickier. Probably the most useful general distinction we can make about effective dialogue is that it never *simply* reproduces conversation for the sake of conversation.

Consider:

"I've got fresh iced tea, if you'd like some."

"I'd love a glass of tea."

"Sugar? Lemon?"

"Just a little lemon, please."

"No problem. I've already got one sliced. Here you go."

"This tastes great. Thanks. It really hits the spot."

"You're welcome."

Question: Is this dialogue believeable? Does it accurately reflect the way people talk?

Answer: Yes, of course.

Question: Does the reader really give a hoot?

Answer: Probably not. Unless, say, the author has tipped off the reader beforehand that the host or hostess has laced the tea pitcher with a few helpings of arsenic.

In other words, quoted conversation without a *subtext* that's important to the outcome of the narrative is just empty words, and wastes the reader's time. Or, as William Sloane puts it in his book *The Craft of Writing:*

> There is a tentative rule that pertains to all fiction dialogue. It must do more than one thing at a time or it is too inert for the purposes of fiction. This may sound harsh, but I consider it an essential discipline.

Not only is Sloane's advice essential, I'd argue, but it applies equally to dialogue in nonfiction, as well.

Fortunately for us as writers, human speech is miraculously good at accomplishing more than one thing at a time.

Perhaps the most basic reason we use speech is to convey important information:

> "Look out! It's falling . . ."
>
> "I need two quarts of motor oil, please."
>
> "Turn left at the next intersection, and the bank is three blocks down on your right."

"If you're lying to me, you're going to be very sorry."

"That ham salad looks a little funny. I wouldn't try it,
if I were you."

In fact, for writing purposes, dialogue is often a much more lively, personal, and revealing way of conveying information than ordinary exposition. That's one reason why storytellers, over the years, have given companions to their main characters: from cowboys to private eyes, the "sidekick" is a revered institution in books and films, as is the more contemporary phenomenon known as the "buddy movie," whether the buddies are male, female, or one of each.

All other things equal, two characters talking to one another are more interesting than the interior monologue of a lone character pondering, mulling, and reflecting. One of the most popular, and effective, ways to advance the action of a story is for a character who's new in town (or at school, or on the job, etc.) to ask questions of somebody who's been around for a while.

But the device of talking-as-exposition has its limits, particularly when the characters who are speaking share a broad base of common knowledge, such as a husband and wife. Consider this exchange:

"Frank, you know I'd love to go with you to the conference in Los Angeles, but I've been working for a whole year on the Junior League Flower Show. Being the chairman, not to mention on the show's tenth anniversary, is a lot of pressure. I can't just walk out and leave everything hanging."

"But honey, it's an important night for *me*, too. I'm giving the keynote speech to the association. It's not like we have to rustle up a babysitter at the last minute; my mom's already planning to keep Abby. And your sister's on the show committee, for gosh sake. Donna could fill in for you, no problem."

Aaaargh, says the reader, at this point. We know that real people don't talk this way. The author's heavy-handed machinery of giving information is clanking so loudly that it distracts us from taking these characters, and their feelings, seriously. They seem one-dimensional, made of cardboard. And not an especially interesting grade of cardboard, at that.

In *real* life, people tend to address their disagreements—no matter how divisive—much more subtly and obliquely:

"You know I'd love to go with you, Frank."

"Oh, sure. You *say* that."

"Yes, I *do* say that. The difference is that in *my* family, we say what we mean."

"I knew you'd drag up my mother again. Any excuse."

"Your mother speaks for herself. She doesn't need excuses."

"Oh, great, honey. I appreciate your warm concern. I appreciate the hell out of it."

Stage director Martha Haarbauer tells her drama students that "a scene is basically an interaction between two characters, each of whom wants a different outcome." That doesn't mean that every conversation in a story has to consist of a no-holds-barred argument, winner take all. The stakes, and the techniques of persuasion, are usually far more subtle. But as a rule, there must be at least a *possibility* of one person changing the other's mind, to even a small degree, in order for the scene to seem real and to have dramatic value for the audience. By contrast, there's this type of exchange:

"You have the power and the influence to level a thousand square miles of this rainforest, Thompson. But what about the people who've lived here for centuries? You'd be destroying their whole way of life."

"Get real, you fool. There's millions to be made here, and if I don't do it, somebody else will."

Regardless of the high stakes, these two guys aren't characters at all—they're just ventriloquist dummies for opposing, and irreconcilable, points of view. In fact, what separates a moving human story from mere propaganda, and what separates a work of serious narrative writing from a melodramatic potboiler or an action comic book, is *the possibility of change in human beings* due to the events in their lives that the story covers. That means acknowledging the possibility for good in even the most evil-hearted villain, and the potential for evil (or cruelty, or compromise, or emotional blind spots) that lurks even within the hero who wears the whitest hat.

Good dialogue, when combined with appropriate action, is perhaps the strongest tool a writer has for creating emotional impact, and for coming to grips with the richness, complexity, and contradictions of the human condition.

To reiterate what William Sloane has told us, dialogue can do several things at once. And the more things it does, the greater the degree to which it carries its own weight and is vital to the context of the surrounding narrative.

Another thing dialogue can do (and exceptionally well) is to illuminate a speaker's personality, character, age, background, social standing, and general outlook on life—all of this independent of any extra clues the author might give us about all those facets, through exposition.

Compare, for example, these four different pieces of dialogue:

"Name isn't enough. I get paid for being careful. What I want to know is, what happens one of the other guns from this bunch gets traced? Am I going to have to start pricing crutches? This is serious business, you know. I don't know who you've been selling to before, but the fellow says you got guns to sell and I need guns. I'm just protecting myself, just being smart . . ."

"As I am no longer in your employment, sir, I can

speak freely without appearing to take a liberty. In my opinion you and Lady Florence were quite unsuitably matched. Her ladyship is of a highly determined and arbitrary temperament, quite opposed to your own. I was in Lord Worplesdon's service for nearly a year, during which time I had ample opportunites of studying her ladyship. The opinion of the servants' hall was far from favourable to her. Her ladyship's temper caused a good deal of adverse comment among us. It was at times quite impossible. You would not have been happy, sir…"

"In walks these three girls in nothing but bathing suits. I'm in the third checkout slot, with my back to the door, so I don't see them until they're over by the bread. The one that caught my eye first was the one in the plaid green two-piece. She was a chunky kid, with a good tan and a sweet broad soft-looking can with those two crescents of white just under it, where the sun never seems to hit, at the top of the backs of her legs. I stood there with my hand on a box of HiHo crackers trying to remember if I rang it up or not. I ring it up again and the customer starts giving me hell. She's one of these cash-register-watchers, a witch about fifty with rouge on her cheekbones and no eye-brows, and I know it made her day to trip me up. She'd been watching cash registers for fifty years and probably never seen a mistake before…"

"Momma, for his sake, asked at the beginning if she

wouldn't be allowed to give some sort of little welcome for Fay—a sitdown tea, I believe she had in mind. And Fay said, 'Oh, please don't bother with a big wholesale reception. That kind of thing was for Becky.' Poor Judge Mac! Because except when it came to picking a wife, he was a pretty worldly old sweet…"

Okay: time for a pop quiz. Judging strictly by the sounds of these voices on the page, without peeking at the answers below, can you determine which of these speakers is (a) a small-time gangster, (b) a proper and reserved British butler, (c) a teenaged boy, and (d) a society matron from a small Southern town?

That wasn't very difficult, was it?

If you guessed that the answers were (a): a, (b): b, (c): c, and (d): d, you scored a hundred percent.

The selections are from, respectively: *The Friends of Eddie Coyle*, a novel by George V. Higgins; "Jeeves Takes Charge," a short story by P.G. Wodehouse; "A & P," a short story by John Updike; and *The Optimist's Daughter*, a novel by Eudora Welty—all of whom, in addition to their other considerable narrative gifts, have an excellent ear for human speech.

That said, let's venture for a moment into some very thorny, but important, territory for writers: the subject of *dialect* in dialogue.

In addition to so-called "standard" English speech (assuming such an animal even exists, in these multicultural times of ours), there are hundreds, if not thousands, of regional and ethnic variations that are known as dialects—with a dialect defined as "A regional variety of a language distinguished by pronunciation, grammar, or vocabulary, especially a variety of speech differing from the standard literary language or speech pattern of the culture in which it exists." In fact, there's an entire branch of academic linguistic study, known as "dialect geography," that records and examines these myriad differences in great detail.

Note the dictionary's three factors that distinguish dialect speech from its more standard brethren: *pronunciation, grammar,* and *vocabulary.*

Let's look at pronunciation, in light of the above dialogue samples. Does a Boston gangster pronounce some of his words differently than a London butler? You bet. How about a New England teenager and an elderly lady from Jackson, Mississippi? Of course.

The traditional way of rendering, in written form, these pronunciation differences is *phonetic spelling*: for instance, "Harvard" becomes "Hah-vad," "widow" becomes "widder," "Thirty-third Street" becomes "Thoity-thoid Street," "New Orleans" becomes "Nawlins," and on and on.

So: if our purpose in writing dialogue is to reproduce, as distinctly as possible, the individual way in which each person speaks, why not go all-out, and spell every individual word the way it *sounds*?

Gosh, I'm glad you asked. I would go so far as to say that phonetically spelled dialogue is one of the most common, and most egregious, offenses of not-yet-published writers—particularly, beginning ones.

I maintain that there's not just one good reason to be wary of over-doing pronunciation, but four—which I'll touch on as briefly as possible, under a general heading that I call "The Uncle Remus Syndrome," drawn from the dialect fables of the popular American humorist Joel Chandler Harris, first published in the 1880s.

Remember Br'er Rabbit's encounter with the Tar-Baby? Here's a refresher:

> "Didn't the fox never catch the rabbit, Uncle Remus?" asked the little boy the next evening.
>
> "He come mighty nigh it, honey, sho's you born, Br'er Fox did. One day atter Br'er Rabbit fool 'im wid dat calamus root, Br'er Fox went ter wuk en got 'im some tar, en mix it wid some turkentime, en fix up a contrapshun w'at he call a Tar-Baby, en he tuck dish yer Tar-Baby an he sot 'er in de big road, en den he lay off in de bushes for to see w'at de news wuz gwine ter be. En he didn't hatter wait long, nudder, kaze bimeby here come Br'er Rabbit pacin' down de road—lippity-clippity, clippity-lippity—dez ez sassy ez a jay-bird . . ."

Okay. Got it? Now, here are some reasons to be very wary of phonetic spellings in dialogue:

(1) They're doggoned hard to read. Instead of sprinting confidently along, concentrating on the images and tone of

the conversation, the reader feels like he or she is walking through (appropriately) warm tar, halting to meticulously dissect each word like the answers to a crossword puzzle.

Admittedly, Joel Chandler Harris is an extreme example. And keep in mind that, for readers of a century or more ago home entertainment consisted of the printed word, supplemented by any music that the members of the family could perform themselves. With the limited attention span of today's audiences, even the most literary ones, a writer who insists on playing hide-and-seek with language is likely to draw the same reaction as some brave soul giving an extended reading of *Finnegan's Wake* to a Chamber of Commerce breakfast club.

(2) Writing phonetic dialogue is not only fun, but addictive. Once you start doing it, you'll almost certainly overdo it. Chandler certainly overdoes it. Read carefully his manufactured words "contrapshun" and "w'at." Can you tell any noticeable difference in sound from the good old standard "contraption" and "what"? Me, either.

(3) The times, they have a-changed. Literary devices go in and out of style. A century or two ago, readers had no problem accepting a know-all, see-all, authorial presence, who addressed them like the voice of God: "Lend an ear, dear reader; the story I'm about to relate is a very sad one, from which you will learn the important moral lessons thus-and-such . . ."

Today, such an approach seems to us quaint and clumsy, only getting in the way of the narrative. Likewise, literature has a long tradition of using strong dialect to tip off the reader that the character in question is of a lower social class and, presumably, less educated than their fellows who speak "standard" English. But in our new millennium, with its spirit of democracy and multiculturalism, that technique just doesn't fly anymore.

Even a number of contemporary writers—Frank O'Connor, for instance—have acknowledged the evolving Zeitgeist by toning down the use of phonetic dialect spellings in new editions of their early writing. As teacher Janet Burroway points out in her textbook *Writing Fiction: A Guide to Narrative Craft,*

> . . . nineteenth-century authors felt free to misspell the dialogue of foreigners, the lower classes, and racial, regional, and ethnic groups. This literary habit persisted into the first decades of the twentieth century. But the world is considerably smaller now, and its consciousness has been raised. Dialect, after all, is entirely relative, and an author who seems unaware of this may sound like a bigot.
>
> The word "bath" pronounced by an Englishman may sound like "bahth" to an American, and pronounced by an American may sound like "banth" to an Englishman. But both know how the word is spelled and resent the implied mockery. Liverpudlians have been knighted; the White house has housed the accents of the Deep South and the Far West; and we resent the implication that regionality equals ignorance.

Does this mean that, henceforth, all of the characters in our writing must "talk like the man on the six-o'clock news" as the lyrics of the country band Alabama put it? Absolutely not. What's at issue is *phonetic spellings*, not word choices or speech patterns. Re-read the four dialogue samples we compared a few pages ago. No reader would mistake one of these characters for another—even though the spellings in all four consist of one hundred percent standard English.

As Burroway goes on, in *Writing Fiction*,

> If you misspell a foreign accent or black English, the reader is likely to have a political rather than a literary reaction. A line of dialogue that runs, "Doan rush me nun, Ah be gwine," reads as caricature, whereas "Don't rush me none, I be going" makes legitimate use of black English syntax and lets us concentrate on the meaning and emotion.

Which leads us to the last, and possibly most important, reason for shunning phonetic dialect unless it's absolutely necessary for clarity:

(4) Pronunciation is *not* the distinguishing difference in regional or ethnic dialects. It's only the tip of the linguistic iceberg. People's mindset, background, and attitudes are mostly conveyed by their *choice* of words and the *order* in which the words are spoken. A writer who ignores this and forges ahead as if dialect were merely fancy spelling comes out looking foolish—as do actors in films who have only a single "stock" accent for each main region of the U.S.,

making all Southerners sound like Li'l Abner, all Westerners like John Wayne, etc.

These butcherings of dialect are especially grating to people who live and work in the area where the real thing is spoken. Each regional dialect has countless sub-regional variations, shadings, and combinations. Authors who are able to recreate those speech patterns faithfully do so not by cerebral cataloging, but by instinct, close listening, and much practice. Mystery writer James Lee Burke, for instance, though nearly all his stories take place in Louisiana, is so attuned to the way people actually talk that the dialects of his characters differ subtly from bayou to bayou, parish to parish.

Two last pieces of advice, and we'll move on:

The best way of learning to write dialect is by example—be on the lookout for, and read repeatedly and closely, authors who seem to you to have an especially good ear for spoken language. Fortunately, these writers are many—Cormac McCarthy, George V. Higgins, Eudora Welty, Russell Banks, Larry Brown, and Josephine Humphreys, just for starters.

Secondly, one of the most effective ways to test your written dialogue is surprisingly easy, and doesn't cost a cent: read it out loud, just as your character would say it if he or she were speaking. It's amazing, how *listening* to speech, as opposed to reading it, highlights any bobbles or rough spots.

And once you've heard them, you can fix them. Make it right. Make it *sing*.

Break a leg.

10

Don't Be a Wallflower:
Throw Down Your 'Crutches'
and Write

L et me tell you a parable about writing. One that really happened. When my son Donovan was learning to walk, he started out the way most people do, I suppose:

He would crawl to the nearest wall, put the palms of both hands against it, and carefully raise himself up to a standing position.

When he got his balance, he would turn sideways and slowly put one foot in front of the other—with one hand still solidly braced against the wall, of course, to keep from falling.

Before long, Donovan could walk up and down the length of any wall like nobody's business. As long as he used one hand to brace with. As his confidence grew, he needed only three fingers to brace with. Then two. Then, just the very tip of his index finger.

With this trick mastered, walking soon became too slow

a means of locomotion for all the business a one-and-a-half-year-old had to transact. In only a day's time, he learned to run—with the all-important fingertip, of course, still touching the wall for safety.

Next, he did research into the principle of corners—namely, how to turn them. By changing the angle of your finger exactly 90 degrees at the right moment, you could keep on running . . . and running. Around all four walls of a room, in fact, picking up speed as you went.

He reminded me of a little blonde-haired bumper car, good to go for hours as long as its thin wire rod was touching the source of electricity up above. He was having the time of his life—cackling, screeching with joy, improvising fancy little stutter-step maneuvers that a college running back would be proud of.

Until, of course, disaster struck: his attention distracted by how much fun he was having, and by the cheers of an appreciative audience, he would glance around and realize that the crucial fingertip had lost contact with the wall. His face would flood with panic, and his little diapered butt would smack the hard floor as if drawn by a magnet.

Defeat. Crying time.

One day, when the inevitable tumble happened, he didn't get sad. He got mad. Wearing an extremely hacked-off expression, he pushed himself to a standing position and started walking with great determination toward the far-off center of the vast, small room. He made it, still standing.

He beamed. He kept walking, all the way to the opposite

wall. He touched it—almost mockingly, I thought—with the tip of his finger. Then he turned around and ran like crazy toward the opposite wall. Repeat. Repeat. And again. I'll never forget the look of freedom and triumph on his face. Take *this*, gravity!

Over the next few years he would wipe out any number of times, both on foot and on wheels, getting bumped and bruised and sometimes a bloody nose, but never again would his life be circumscribed by where a wall happened to be located.

The End.

The reason I bring up this story is because I vividly remember the day I realized—after spending some twenty-plus years of teaching writers' workshops—that of all the people who had told me, in one-on-one conferences, that they passionately wanted to publish their writing, more than half of them came into class with certified reasons why they would never be able to reach that goal.

The individual variations were endless, but the basic themes were remarkably consistent.

One of the most frequently used crutches is this one:

—*"I have amazing stories to tell, but they would hurt my family's feelings, so I can't write them until everybody in my family but me is dead."* Or, its companion worry, *"What about libel? What if somebody sues me?"*

Your worries are over. One of the most wonderful aspects of fiction is that, in writing it, you can draw both on your personal experiences *and your imagination* to create a world and characters that are, as William Faulkner once put it, "Truer than mere truth." What Faulkner considered "mere truth" are the outward, literal facts of a situation: people's names, facial appearances, body types, hometowns, etc.

Was your childhood made a living hell by a father who was a railroad man, tall and athletic, who collected guns? So make him a short, swarthy construction boss whose passion is woodworking. Then tell the story. Nobody will know the difference.

Were you raised by a cruel, dotty aunt from an old New Orleans family, who always dressed as if she were going to a funeral? Make her an older cousin, who married money in Nashville and then gave the guy a heart attack. As long as you change the identifiable physical details of a person or a situation, what would anybody have to gain by coming forward and claiming that a sadistic, crazy, or felonious character is actually them in disguise?

Another popular non-writing crutch:

—*"I have so many great ideas, but the stories all happen in faraway places I've never been, and I don't have the time or money to travel there and do the research."*

Try telling that to Emily Dickinson, who wrote, "There is no frigate like a book, to take us worlds away…" Well-written books can literally bring foreign places to life for us, without us having to travel there physically. So can feature films and documentaries. History is full of good and popular writers who never lived in the locales they wrote about. All great stories, William Faulkner told us, are about "the human heart in conflict with itself." If your people are believable and intriguing to the reader, their surroundings will be, too—even if you've gotten a feel for the place second-hand, through books.

Plus, most writers and researchers haven't yet fully absorbed what a tremendous boon the Internet has become for sharing information. Many times, in recent years, I've had a detailed question about geographical or cultural matters that I couldn't find the answer to in traditional reference sources. So, I went straight to the horse's mouth—posting a note on a relevant Internet newsgroup or bulletin board. Within a day or so, I was corresponding directly with someone who actually lived in the area.

I'm continually amazed at how eager people are to help with writing projects—whether they themselves are writers or not. At times, I've asked a question in the evening (American time) and awakened the next morning to find an E-mail with all the information I needed: and often, illustrated by a snapshot from a digital camera as well. All for the $20 or so monthly fee of an Internet connection, without ever contacting a travel agent.

The global village is here. Use and enjoy it.

Then, there's the non-writing crutch that swings both ways: *"Nobody will publish what I write, because it's too (insert either 'clean and moral', or 'filthy and depraved').*

That excuse won't fly. Never before has a wider range of

subjects been available on the world's bookshelves. Never before have so many specialized periodicals been clamoring for the types of material their particular audiences are attuned to. And that's not even counting the growing market for "E-books" and other online publications.

Religious fiction and nonfiction regularly make bestseller lists. So does erotica, and extreme material whose detractors call "pornography" or at least "in bad taste." There is no conspiracy, either right-wing or left-wing, to keep your writing from getting published. Of course, there's competition—but never lose sight of the fact that an audience exists for anything that you, as a writer, can make *fresh and interesting* to a reader. Period.

But even established authors will tell you that writing is not someplace you "arrive," but is rather a lifetime apprenticeship. You learn to write by writing. The more you write, the better you get.

Which brings us to what's probably the most pervasive non-writing excuse of all:

  — *"I desperately want to write, but I just don't have the time. Maybe, someday . . ."*

Listen up. Two of the many hard, cold facts of life that every thinking adult needs to know are (a) there is no Easter bunny, and (b) there is no such thing as "time to write." Every moment we spend not eating or sleeping (or even if we are), the world makes an endless quota of demands on our time.

We all daydream of being transported to some remote

villa, in a bare room without phone or fax, where we could rapturously spend weeks at a time with no imperative but to write what we've always wanted to write.

In the first place, very few people ever achieve that blessed state. Even more importantly, a fact of human nature rears its ugly head: if you currently have even a short period of time each day in which you could be working on your writing apprenticeship, but find some excuse not to, you would find equally valid excuses for not writing even if you were transported to some distraction-free paradise.

Can you somehow carve out, in your current circumstance, as little as fifteen minutes a day to sit in a room alone and put words on paper? If so, you can write the first draft of a short story or essay in a matter of a couple of months. A hefty novella in six months. A fair-sized novel in a year or less.

The most important thing you can ever do for your development as a writer is setting aside, however brief, an inviolable block of time each day to do the daunting and usually unglorious work of putting one word in front of another. Writing is not only a skill, but a habit. If your brain knows that it's going to be stuck staring at a blank page or empty computer screen for a certain period of time anyhow, it gives up the fight and begins working—even unconsciously, when the top of your mind isn't even thinking of writing—on coming up with some words to fill that space of time. The hardest part is making the commitment.

One of my favorite novelists first tried her hand at

writing fiction when she was (a) a full-time social worker, and (b) first-time mother of an infant daughter. The only moments of the day she could claim for herself was during her daughter's night-time feeding. While the baby fed, the mother jotted words in longhand on a legal pad. Eventually the words became a short story. And another. And eventually one of them sold to a magazine. That was about fifteen years ago. In the meantime she's published four novels, is working on a fifth, and teaches a popular writing workshop at a local university.

Every writer has to start somewhere. The only place any of us can start is, pardon my grammar, the place we're already at. And the only time is today.

Why not throw down your crutches—your well-worn excuses for *not* writing—and run toward the middle of the big, empty room of your imagination that you've been circling for so long with one fingertip to the wall of reason and safety?

True, you might fall on your rear. Any number of times. But, you might dance. And dance. Like nobody's business.

11

The 'Telegram Syndrome': Catching Words That Swing Both Ways

Most of us have heard the (okay, maybe apocryphal) story about the cheapskate press agent, during the golden days of Hollywood, who tried to save money by wiring to a movie studio the abbreviated question, "HOW OLD CARY GRANT?"

To which the studio supposedly replied, "OLD CARY GRANT FINE. HOW YOU?"

The nearest equivalent of the telegrammatic writing style that survives today is the lowly and ubiquitous newspaper headline. Though good headline writers bring much skill and experience to their craft, most of us don't really pay attention to a headline unless the writer screws it up.

Sure enough, there's no shortage of authentic howlers. Just run the phrase "goofy headlines" through any search engine and see what turns up:

—SURVIVOR OF SIAMESE TWINS JOINS PARENTS

——SQUAD HELPS DOG BITE VICTIM

——TEACHER STRIKES IDLE KIDS

——PRESIDENT WINS ON BUDGET, BUT MORE LIES AHEAD

——SOVIET VIRGIN LANDS SHORT OF GOAL AGAIN

——IRAQUI HEAD SEEKS ARMS

——LUNG CANCER IN WOMEN MUSHROOMS

——DEAF MUTE GETS NEW HEARING IN COURT

——PROSTITUTES APPEAL TO POPE

——RED TAPE HOLDS UP NEW BRIDGE

——MINERS REFUSE TO WORK AFTER DEATH

——NEVER WITHHOLD HERPES FROM LOVED ONE

——2 SISTERS REUNITED AFTER 18 YEARS IN CHECKOUT LINE

But you don't have to be a headline writer to accidentally run afoul of the "Telegram Syndrome"; a reader's misinterpretation of a phrase can happen because of the richness and flexibility of the English language—namely, the fact that the same word can serve as two, three, or more different parts of speech.

In a headline, that possibility for confusion is magnified because such helpful clues as articles, modifiers, and certain verb forms are omitted for the sake of space and immediacy.

Even if you don't write headlines, words with multiple personalities that occur in your prose can be a momentary bump in the road for your reader. Most such bumps are easily cleared up by a few seconds of thought and re-reading. But as we've noted before, *any* accidental road-bump for a reader is a bad thing. The best writing is *seamless* writing.

Minor irritations tend to accumulate for a reader—consciously or not—and enough of them can lead to your piece of prose being laid aside for something more appealing.

That's why, as part of your final, fine-tooth comb revisions, it can be helpful to give one quick, objective read-through of your work with an eye out specifically for words that could be interpreted as more than one part of speech.

Nouns that are also verbs are a major culprit, as the headlines above show:

Join can be either a transitive or intransitive verb, for instance. *Land* can be both verb and subject and, in some cases, modifier, as in "land troops." The same goes for *strike, bite, mushroom, help, lie,* ad infinitum.

Likewise, a phrase such as *hold up* not only can serve as a verb or noun, but can have meanings as diverse as "to delay," "to support," and "to rob from."

These chameleon words and phrases can be hard to ferret out of one's own writing, because the person who writes the piece retains the basic context of all its usages at some level of memory, even after laying the writing aside (a highly recommended practice, by the way, if deadlines permit) for several days or more.

For me, at least, it's much easier to spot potential turn-coat words and phrases if you make them the *sole focus* of a single read-through, and if work yourself into a sort of cranky, devil's advocate frame of mind for the duration. (If you're one of us who naturally become—unsought and unwanted—a cranky devil's advocate during certain periods of time, you can at least put the episode to good use by saving up some work that needs combing through to eliminate the telegram syndrome.)

Here's one I recently culled from my own writing, an essay about the Thanksgiving meals I had as a child:

> There was turkey and ham and a hen for the oven, dressing with onions, and a whole stovetop of stewing vegetables.

Just how did the hen get *into* the room where the onions were dressing, anyway? And are the onions male or female, and does it matter?

To amend the notion that "dressing" in this case might be intended as a verb rather than a noun, I revised the sentence as follows:

> There was turkey and ham and a hen for the oven, sage-flavored dressing with onions, and a whole stovetop of stewing vegetables.

There are any number of other ways to have solved the same problem, including:

> There was turkey and ham, and a hen for the oven. There was dressing with onions, and a whole stovetop of stewing vegetables.

Ideally, your choice should boil down to a revision that (a) does the job in the simplest way, without being obtrusive in its new construction, and (b) is in keeping with the *pacing* and *rhythms* of the surrounding sentences (See Chapter 2).

Here's a telegram-syndrome goof I caught recently in a radio news broadcast:

> The lawyers have until eleven a.m. Friday to file their briefs.

This gave me pause. Could the lawyers use a simple fingernail file on their underwear, I wondered, or would the judge require the big, industrial-strength type of file?

Here's an improved version:

> The lawyers have until eleven a.m. Friday to file the briefs.

Taking away the possessive "their" makes a reader less likely to envision underwear, I think. But, since the purpose of the legal briefs has been explained earlier in the article, a better solution might be:

> The lawyers have until eleven a.m. Friday to file those briefs.

If such concerns strike you as picky and penny-ante, you're at least half right—if, by "picky," you mean not being at the very top of a writer's concerns. That's why they occupy the next-to-last tool...er, chapter...in this tool kit. Where tuning is concerned, consider these "fine" to "very fine."

But penny-ante? I think not.

When it comes to clarity in writing, John Gardner's dictum (See Chapter 3) that "The meaning of a sentence should be as obvious as a grizzly bear in a well-lighted kitchen" seems to me a very worthy goal.

Although such momentary incidences of word confusion are quickly set aright by a reader, those blips on the screen of seamless attention certainly don't do any good for the reader's overall experience of your work. At the risk of co-opting the jargon of quality controllers in manufacturing and of get-tough-on-crime advocates, the best policy for a writer where potential word mixups are concerned is "zero tolerance."

⊷⊷⊙⊜⊶⊶

One Last Thing:

Advertising may fuel the engine of our national economy, but ad copy is just as responsible as journalistic headlines for using awkward, and/or misleading, grammatical constructions.

My own pet peeve, inculcated into me by talented and vigorous newspaper editor Clarke Stallworth, is the misuse of "over" and "under," as in "Over 10,000 Units Sold!" or "Under 25 Percent Expected to Vote."

The rule is a clear-cut one:

— "Over" and "under" refer to *relative positions in physical space*.

— "More than" and "fewer/less than" refer to *amounts and quantities*.

In other words, a flag may fly *over* those 10,000 units of merchandise, but *fewer* than 25 percent of those people are expected to vote.

Sure, it's a minor infraction in the big picture, but where writing is concerned, every bit of clarity helps. And Clarke and I thank you.

12

Expelling Gremlins:
Getting the 'Accidents' Out

If you've faithfully applied the first eleven tools in the *Tool Kit* to your manuscript, its narrative engine should be humming along quite nicely. But before you turn that engine loose on the public, one last fine-tuning is in order.

Every published writer knows the sinking, egg-on-face feeling of discovering in a finished piece one or more accidental, clunker phrases—now preserved for all posterity— that neither the writer nor editor(s) caught before the manuscript went into print.

Often, these accidents revolve around double meanings. Say that you're reading along in a crime novel (whose author shall remain nameless, for courtesy's sake), and there's an extended shoot-out between the good guys and bad guys— bullets flying everywhere, and bodies hitting the dirt. Suddenly, a backup squad car arrives on the scene:

The driver killed the engine.

A little extreme, don't you think? Couldn't he just have shut off the ignition, and let it go at that?

Likewise, many commonly used phrases can be either literal or metaphorical, depending on the context.

"Get outta here!" can be, depending on the tone and the speaker, an expression of incredulity or an order to vacate the premises post-haste.

"You're killing me…" can be a compliment on a great joke, or…well, you get the idea. Make sure that the context of such comments is crystal-clear.

At the opposite end of the clunker spectrum are redundancies: making things *too* clear.

The aforementioned crime novel, for instance, also contains this line:

> "Damn you! I'll have you prosecuted!" he said, angrily.

As if he could have said it *sweetly*.

A few adverbs go a very long way in a piece of writing. Avoid them by making words or actions specific enough that they don't require modification.

Also good to avoid are the cloying array of verbs that writers sometimes dredge up as alternatives to "said."

"Spat," "hissed," and "croaked" are perfectly good terms if your story takes place in the middle of a zoo, but as dialogue tags for human speakers, they have the definite air of purple prose about them. It's hard to improve on the time-honored "he said" and "she said," with the occasional shout or whisper when the volume level is crucial to the speaker's context.

Another category of clunker that's easy to overlook if you're in a rush is the accidental repetition, rhyming, or near-rhyming, of words in a sentence. From our anonymous snakebitten crime novel comes this example:

> *The black pack crackled as he extracted a cigarette.*

Try saying *that* three times, real fast.

Examples abound from other sources, too:

> The report contained nothing about how much damage was sustained.
>
> On the corner stood a grubby-looking man who looked to be a vagrant.
>
> Spots passed across her field of vision. She had a vision of her parents at home, wondering where she was.
>
> "Are you sure you don't have an ulterior motive?" he asked, with a superior air.
>
> Feeling suspicious, he took a surreptitious look.
>
> The jury, shortly after being sequestered, requested more information.

Some wise person once said, "Everything about a piece of writing must look as if it were done on purpose." Sloppiness is a definite no-no. Most readers, whether consciously or not, are willing to invest their reading time in proportion to their sense of how well the author has invested his/her time—not in the sense of being laborious or over-thorough, but of having not taken short-cuts or left any loose threads dangling.

Finally, there's the kind of writing gremlin that might best be described as the verbal equivalent of a facial tic: the repeated use of a word, phrase, or device without recognizing your repetition. One of the most common of these "tics" is to string along adjective/noun pairs in such a predictable way that sentences come to have a sing-song element:

> Out on the wide fields, brown grouse ran and yellow butterflies fluttered about the tall grass in the bright sun, as puffy clouds bloomed in a blue sky and a warm breeze blew on the children's upturned faces.

There are any number of ways of alternating the phrasing so as to avoid the awkward symmetry of adjective/noun, adjective/noun. One possibility is:

> The grouse running in the wide fields were as brown as tree bark. Yellow butterflies fluttered about the knee-high grass, and the playing children took it all in: the hard blue sky with its mountain of cumulus, the breeze warm on their faces.

Another common mannerism is to fall into the spell of inserting too many qualifiers into your writing: *almost, it was nearly as if, a sort of, not quite, almost as though, virtually, the equivalent of,* etc. Subtlety is all well and good, but too much of it can make a writer come across as hesitant, as trying to hedge his/her bets. When that happens, take a closer look at the metaphors, images, or declarations that these qualifiers qualify, and see if they can be fine-tuned so as to make the qualifier unnecessary.

There. We've taken the engine of your story and tuned it up with all twelve major tool groups, from coarse to fine and in between. Running smoother now? Good.

It's time to give your narrative vehicle one final pat, for luck—and then take it out on the road.

A Writer's Tool Kit has a companion web site at http://www.writerstoolkit.com